Coming to Terms

A Mother's Story

I0103273

Arlene Hindle

chipmunkapublishing

the mental health publisher

Arlene Hindle

Published by

Chipmunkapublishing

PO Box 6872

Brentwood

Essex CM13 1ZT

United Kingdom

http://www.chipmunkapublishing.com

Copyright © Arlene Hindle 2011

Edited by Aleks Lech

Chipmunkapublishing gratefully acknowledge the support of Arts Council England.

Author Biography

Arlene Hindle has written an account of the harrowing road her son, Peter, her husband and she travelled on the road leading to Peter's eventual diagnosis of Bipolar Disorder, his treatment and gradual recovery to a stable condition.

She decided to write the story for a number of reasons. Firstly to raise awareness in the family as the complaint can be genetic. Secondly to encourage others to persevere through any visible signs of the illness and the difficulties that can ensue, for Bipolar Disorder can, in most cases be managed successfully. Thirdly, in the hope that writing the story would be an emotional release for her.

Arlene is a retired nurse and lives in Harrogate, North Yorkshire. She enjoys reading, walking in the Dales and occasionally writes for the Harrogate, Tapes for Blind.

Arlene Hindle

Synopsis

An account of the pain inflicted on sufferers of manic depression (Bipolar Disorder), their family and those around them.

'Peter was with us for 6 weeks. At first it was like having a stranger in the house. He was so quiet. But we gave him his space to do as he pleased... He was a lost soul and all we could do was wait patiently and hope that the Prozac would eventually take effect.'

'...We were somewhat taken aback when Peter phoned at the beginning of May to tell us that he had 'popped the question' and that they were getting engaged. He had known her for just six weeks.'

'The letters were unpaid bills, final demands to the tune of hundreds of pounds, so our fears over Peter's inability to manage his financial affairs were fully realised as we sat at our table that day. Sarah looked across at Peter in a state of incredulous disbelief.'

'Dr Darwood was sitting, almost silhouetted, his back to the window, behind an enormous desk piled high with papers and patients' notes. I took a deep breath and then said 'I have come to see you because my husband and I are very seriously concerned about Peter. He is not getting any better and this has gone on for far too long.''

'The night Peter came home drunk was the first of many.'

'...Then he would begin his binge drinking at our village pub. The pub was just a couple of hundred yards from our home and he would walk home from there.'

'The psychiatrist said 'Young man, you look like an out of work undertaker. When I have finished with you, you will be playing football and chasing the girls again.'

'Peter was discharged and back home with us at the end of the 3rd week in January. We had hoped that he might have been easier to live with, but were disappointed, for the only real difference we could see was that he was no longer drinking.'

'The first thing I noticed was the raw red scald over his eye.'

Coming to Terms

This is Arlene Hindle's first book, written from her personal experiences when she and her husband John supported their eldest son Peter through a long illness, eventual diagnosis of Bipolar Disorder and a gradual recovery to stability.

She trained as a nurse at the Norfolk and Norwich Hospital and worked for twenty five years in a variety of nursing roles.

Now retired, Arlene occasionally writes for Tapes for the Blind in the Harrogate area of North Yorkshire and enjoys reading and walking in the Dales.

She has a second son, five grandchildren and three step-grandchildren.

Arlene Hindle

INTRODUCTION

Peter, our eldest son, was diagnosed as having Bipolar Disorder in 1995.

The harrowing road Peter, my husband and I travelled and the events leading up to his diagnosis are as clear in my mind as though it all happened yesterday.

I had often toyed with the idea of writing Peter's story, but could never decide when, where or how to begin. Somehow there had to be a trigger.

I had made many notes and felt that they should be compiled into a written story for three reasons.

Firstly, to raise awareness of the disorder for our family, as Bipolar Disorder can prove to be genetic. Secondly, to encourage others to persevere through any visible signs of the illness occurring, and finally, in the hope that the writing of the story would be an emotional release for me.

Nothing ever materialised until seven years ago.

Through a friend, I received an invitation to join a writing group being formed by a Barbara Roberts. The group was to be called 'Lifelines' and its purpose was for members to study and record parts of their family histories for grandchildren and future generations.

Joining seven others, the group was established under Barbara's leadership. A gifted writer, her expertise and encouragement was an inspiration to us all. We valued her greatly, hanging on to every word as she read us many of her own memoirs.

Membership of the group was the trigger. When Barbara first read my notes she said 'You must write this. Even the bones of the story make good reading.' And so I began.

Sadly Barbara died a year ago, but she is sorely missed and lives on through Lifelines.

This book is dedicated to her and the members of the Lifelines group. For without their help and encouragement, it might never have been written.

CHAPTER 1

I dreamed I was walking along the banks of the river that runs through the valley and the village where we live.

It was a dull, grey day, the kind soon forgotten, its only purpose seeming to be to exaggerate the better sunny days in between.

Unusually for this popular part of the village, there wasn't a soul about.

The river was running quite low that day, but as I walked on, I noticed at one point that the water had become crystal clear, and the river bed shelved dramatically to a depth of some eight feet or more. My curiosity drew me nearer to the water's edge.

Dreams have a way of manipulating and stretching our minds and imagination, far beyond anything that we might perceive in our waking hours, and this dream was no exception. For there, sitting down under the water, on the river bed of large pebbles, was a little boy of perhaps two years of age.

He wasn't moving, fighting for breath, or even trying to escape, but was just sitting there, looking up at me, with large beseeching eyes. Beside him in the water, as though somehow protecting him, was a large seal.

I was completely transfixed by the sight for what seemed to be a long, long time, before I dived into the water to rescue the child. Gathering him into my arms I made for the surface, the seal slowly and smoothly gliding away, its purpose apparently now over.

The child was beautiful and I sat there on the river bank, holding him close and studying his face, as he continued to look up at me with those huge pleading eyes. At first he seemed to be most perfect in every way, but I then noticed, as my eyes moved down from his little face, that something was terribly wrong.

One of his legs was trapped in what appeared to be a large milk bottle. The neck of the bottle reached to just below the knee and from there, right down to the ankle, was a large open bleeding wound.

Consumed with panic, I started to run with all my might, with the child in my arms. Then suddenly, I was in a huge casualty department. The place was in a state of utter bedlam. Patients were lying around everywhere on stretchers; doctors and nurses were rushing about trying to cope with the chaos, but failing miserably.

I tried desperately to get help for the little boy, but everyone was deliberately avoiding eye contact and quite categorically ignoring me. I panicked and started to scream. Still no one would look at me. I screamed again and again but it made no difference.

All the time, the child lay back in my arms, looking up at me.

By now, utterly distraught, I broke down and began to cry uncontrollably.

It was then that I felt someone gently tapping my shoulder, and before I could turn to see who it was, I heard my mother's voice, saying, 'Look Arlene. Look at his leg now.'

I looked down and what I then saw woke me from my dream. For the little leg, although still trapped in the bottle, had now stopped bleeding, but all the flesh had fallen away from the bone.

The shock of what I saw woke me.

Coming to Terms

I lay awake analysing the dream, and although I reached my conclusions in a very short space of time, the memory of that sequence of events, leading up to the macabre sight I finally saw, will forever linger in my mind.

I have always believed that the dream was a very significant turning point in my life. Realisation dawned that night that my denial was over.

I had saved that little boy's life, but he would never, ever be the same again.

I had come to terms.

CHAPTER 2

My husband John and I have moved several times over the years and had spent the last fourteen of them living in Brighton. In 1988, with our pending retirement in mind, we moved to Yorkshire where we were both born and where our hearts were.

We bought a house in the country with a wonderful view over the river and the hills beyond. We enjoyed gardening, walking in the Dales, involvement in village life and the company of new friends.

John was still working as a management consultant and, being very successful, was still travelling quite extensively. He loved the work but was looking forward to joining me in retirement and having time to enjoy and develop new hobbies.

I had retired from nursing a few months previously. Finding work wherever we lived had always been relatively easy, and I had always managed to manoeuvre my working life around running our family home. I too had enjoyed my job, but the time had come to step down, collect my thoughts and adapt to a very different way of life.

Peter, 29 years old, the elder of our two sons, was still living in Brighton, working for a large printing company. He started working there as an office boy, gradually working his way up the career ladder and gaining qualifications. He eventually became one of the company's most successful employees and sales representatives. It had been pleasing to see him grow in confidence as he had always been rather self-effacing at school, even though he was very bright, and would worry about the least thing, so he well deserved his success.

He loved sport, played squash, tennis and football, had a

wide circle of friends and was very popular, partly we imagined because of his zest for life and his sense of humour. He was buying his own flat and enjoying life to the full when John and I moved away.

Michael, three years younger than Peter, couldn't have been more different. He had always sailed through life without a care in the world and nothing fazed him. He had obtained an art degree and on leaving college had been quite determined to work for no one but himself. Putting painting on hold, he liked working with wood and set about making and selling wooden board games and similar items. He and his partner Zoe had recently moved down to Cornwall, supposedly an artist's paradise. There they lived a Bohemian lifestyle, happily scratching a living, hoping one day to make their fortune.

Despite their very different characters and lifestyles the two brothers were regularly in touch with one another and it had always been a source of pleasure to John and I that as well as being brothers, they were the greatest of friends.

We had always been very fortunate and our family life was very happy. Despite the change in the pattern of our lives when we moved away from Brighton, the future looked promising and we all appeared to have much to look forward to.

Or so we believed.

CHAPTER 3

November 1992

I was convalescing at home after having had a hysterectomy two weeks previously. I was still very weak but enjoying a gentle routine in order to regain my strength.

John had just come back from a couple of working days away and we had settled down by the fire with a coffee after our evening meal, when the phone rang.

John answered and learning that it was Peter, responded in his usual jovial fatherly manner, but that came to an abrupt end and the smile faded from his face as he listened to what Peter had to say.

'I'm so sorry, Peter' he said moments later. 'But why haven't you told us before?'

He listened on, frowning as he absorbed all that Peter was saying. I got up and walked over to him, anxious to know what the call was all about and wanting to talk to Peter myself. But John held up his hand to reassure me, looking at me solemnly as he did so, then said,

'Try not to worry Peter. It will pass. I'll talk to your Mum and we'll get back to you very soon.' He then, deep in thought, carefully put down the receiver. We both sat down again and I braced myself as John poured us more coffee, then began.

'Peter seems to have had some sort of breakdown...'

'What?' was all I could say, I was so taken aback.

Peter had been to stay with us just two months previously. We had all had a thoroughly good few days together, walking in the Dales, eating out, and enjoying an evening at the theatre.

Just before coming to us, Peter had been head-hunted and offered a job with a bigger firm. He was looking forward to starting with them when he got back. When he left us he was fine.

John sat frowning, slowly stirring his coffee.

'What is it John? What's brought this about?'

John slowly shook his head.

'He's been off work for almost a month. Says the new job is stressful and he can't cope.'

'But why didn't he tell us before?'

'He didn't want us to know because you've been in hospital. He's been to the doctor and is on some sort of medication but doesn't feel that it's making any difference.'

'He must feel he needs some support or he wouldn't have phoned us.'

We both sat for what seemed an age, saying nothing, trying to take it in.

I knew exactly what would be going through John's mind.

His brother had committed suicide a few years previously, leaving a wife and four young children. Although he had been prone to moods, the family had been mystified as to why he had taken his life. There had been no suicide note.

A short while later, keen to break John's train of thought, and convinced that there was only one solution, I walked over to John's chair, picked up the phone and dialled

Peter's number.

'Hello' he said. I barely recognised his dull, toneless voice.

'Hello Peter, it's Mum. I'm sorry you're not well, love. Why don't you come up and stay with us for a couple of weeks? The change might help. A bit of company.

There was a long pause.

'I don't know.'

'You know I would come down there if I was strong enough. Your Dad is as busy as ever. If you don't feel you can drive you could come up by train.'

Again,

'I don't know.'

'If you came up here you can help me and we can look after each other.'

I waited.

'I'll think about it Mum, if that's what you want.'

'Yes I do, Peter.'

'I'll get your dad to look up the train times and sort it out with you.'

Then not wanting to prolong the call in case he decided against the idea, I said 'Bye for now Peter' and put the phone down.

A while later John phoned Peter back with various train schedules and, speaking gently and carefully to him, suggested that he would pick him up at Leeds station at three o'clock the following afternoon.

Again, Peter was slow in responding, but he reluctantly agreed to come.

I studied John's face as he sipped his coffee, then, seeming to shrug off his thoughts, he looked across at me.

'I suppose you're right, if you feel you can manage. He likes coming up here. It might just make a difference'.

Convinced that we had made the right decision, and thankful that Peter would be with us the next day, we eventually went to bed shaken, but without the slightest doubt in our minds that we would soon have Peter well again.

The following morning John made a couple of telephone calls to re-arrange his diary and then left to keep an appointment. I carefully paced myself as I made up a bed for Peter and prepared a meal for his arrival. As I was settling down to a sandwich at lunchtime the phone rang.

I was taken by surprise as it was Peter.

'It's me, Mum.' There was a long pause. 'I'm not coming.'

'But where are you Peter?'

I eased myself down into a chair.

'But why have you changed your mind?'

'I couldn't get on the train.'

'But why not?'

'I couldn't do it. I just stood and watched the train pull away. I didn't even buy a ticket.'

'Perhaps coming today was too short notice for you.'

'It's not that Mum. Please understand. I couldn't do it. I just couldn't do it. I've come back home.'

He waited for me to say something more but the shock of realising that he was far worse than I had thought got the better of me and I broke down in tears.

'Please Peter' I pleaded.

He must have heard the break in my voice.

'Don't cry Mum.'

'Please come up and see us. Let your dad and I help you.'

I was furious with myself for losing control but I had few reserves at that time, although it did prove to be a catalyst and move Peter's thoughts from himself. For after yet another long pause he said 'All right Mum. I'll come tomorrow.'

Before I could say another word, he put the telephone down.

And he came.

I was very badly shaken when he came through the door and walked towards me the following afternoon.

Peter is a good-looking young man of medium height and is solidly built. He has large, expressive hazel eyes and a head of thick brown hair.

But that day there were deep shadows under his eyes, his hair was in need of a cut and he was unshaven. His shoulders seemed to droop and it was as though he had no strength in his arms as he half-heartedly hugged me.

Coming to Terms

'Hello Mum.'

'Hello Peter. I'm so glad to see you.' I swallowed hard.

'Have you had a good journey?'

'It was OK I suppose.'

'Would you like some tea?'

'No thanks Mum. I'm all right.' With that he picked up his bag and walked down the hall and up the stairs.

John and I went into the kitchen and as he helped me lay the table for dinner, he told me that Peter had hardly said a word to him in the car on the way home. We heard Peter unpacking then showering in the bathroom. When he reappeared he looked better, but just nodded to us at the door, before walking through to the lounge.

I followed him and watched as he sat down, folded his arms, put his head back and within seconds was sound asleep. The simple journey had completely exhausted him.

Later at dinner John and I talked to one another quietly in an attempt to break the otherwise painful silence. Peter picked away at his food not saying a word. He eventually pushed his plate away, sat back and shook his head.

'I'm sorry Mum. I can't.'

'It's all right Peter. It doesn't matter.'

'I just don't know why I feel like this. I've worked hard but don't seem to be getting anywhere. Work hasn't been a problem before. I have no patience with people and my boss says I've been morose.'

'Do you think the job is too big for you?' asked John,

carefully.

'I don't know. I was always so confident but it's all gone. I told my boss I was seeing the doctor because I didn't feel right and he's prepared to give me a chance. I'm avoiding my friends. My flat's in a terrible state and I dread the thought of going back to work.'

Tears began to spill down his cheeks.

'I'm afraid of losing my job.'

I handed Peter a tissue and John and I looked at one another as he cried. Two minds with one thought. Peter would come through this, but it would take much more than a couple of weeks with us for him to do so.

I managed to arrange an emergency appointment and temporary registration for Peter with our own GP the following morning. It emerged that Peter had been prescribed Prozac three weeks previously and had been advised to take the medication for two months. Our GP recommended that Peter should give it more time to take effect.

Peter was with us for 6 weeks. At first it was like having a stranger in the house, he was so quiet. But we gave him his space to do as he pleased. He slept late and would always unnecessarily apologise for doing so, for he was constantly weary. His appetite was poor but I felt that he was probably eating rather more with us than when he had been alone. He passed the days reading and watching TV, but his concentration span was short so he would often take himself off for walks. His brother Mike phoned him regularly but Peter had little to say. He contacted his manager in Brighton who appeared to be sensitive and encouraging and reassured Peter that he would be glad to have him back at work as soon as he was well enough. This gave Peter the lift and boost he so badly needed.

Coming to Terms

Even so, he was a lost soul and all we could do was wait patiently and hope that the Prozac would eventually take effect.

It was after Peter had been with us for almost three weeks that we began to see a change. An occasional smile would slip through and his appetite improved. He took the bus into town one day and had his hair cut, borrowed my library ticket and came back with a couple of books. It was a start. He began to take an interest in all that was happening around him and almost overwhelming me with kindness, would help me with food shopping and then occasionally cook John and I an evening meal. He was much more talkative with his brother when he phoned and also began contacting his friends in Brighton. Finally, as though to underline our huge relief that he was better, he phoned his boss in Brighton to let him know that he would be back at work at the beginning of January.

Pleased that his brother was better, and knowing that John and I might need a quiet Christmas, Mike invited Peter to spend Christmas in Cornwall with him and Zoe. Peter hesitated at first but it didn't take long for us to persuade him that some young company was just what he needed. Our suggestion worked and Peter travelled down by train. There were no problems this time.

He telephoned us almost daily from there and reassured us that he was feeling much better, although we could tell that by his tone of voice. One day when Mike and Zoe were particularly busy he took himself off for a long walk along the coast, feeling the need to be alone and collect his thoughts. Peter told us later that the walk had been a wonderful therapy and a final turning point in his recovery. He travelled home to Brighton from Cornwall.

Peter returned to work quite happily in the New Year and during the following weeks his medication was gradually reduced, then discontinued.

Arlene Hindle

By the beginning of February 1993 he was fine again and back on track.

24

CHAPTER 4

March - October 1993

Two months later, Peter's new job was going well. I had fully recovered from my operation. We had just got back from a fortnight's holiday, when the following morning the phone rang. It was Peter.

'Hello Mum' he said. 'I've got some great news. I met a girl called Sarah at a party. She's ever so pretty and clever too. She's a Geneticist. Works at Guys in London. I want you and Dad to meet her. We're in love Mum. I've never felt like this before.' He barely paused for breath, such was his enthusiasm. I opened my mouth to speak but clearly wasn't going to get a word in edgeways.

'She has to come up to Leeds University next Friday for part of a research project she's working on. I'm going to drive her up there. We could all meet up. Shame Mike's so far away. What do you think, Mum?'

I smiled to myself. This was all such a contrast to the way he had been a few weeks previously.

'I think it's wonderful news, Peter. I'm very happy for you.'

'What do you think about us meeting up?'

'It's a lovely idea. Your Dad is as busy as ever but we'll see what we can do and phone you back tonight.'

'That would be brilliant. Oh by the way I nearly forgot. Did you have a good holiday?'

'Yes thanks.'

'Good. 'Bye for now.' And he hung up.

John chuckled as I related to him Peter's telephone call. He managed to reshuffle his diary so that we were able to meet Peter and Sarah at a hotel in Leeds the following Friday afternoon.

Sarah was indeed a pretty girl.

She had a head of beautiful shoulder-length, blonde, wavy hair, big, blue eyes and a lovely, ready smile. After the first pleasantries of introductions and urged along by Peter, she told us about her work at Guys and that she was studying for a PhD in Genetics. She was easy company and we could see why Peter was so taken with her. Without doubt, the attraction was mutual. They held hands and kept gazing adoringly at one another throughout our time together. John and I drove home feeling pleased and happy for Peter, and although they had only known each other for a very short space of time, we thought Sarah might well be good for Peter if first impressions were anything to go by.

During the weeks that followed, Peter's enthusiasm never waned and he would frequently phone and give us an update on how things were going. Sarah was living in London at that time but they would get together at weekends and enjoy a good social life with their many friends. At Easter, Mike and Zoe, keen to meet Sarah, invited us all to spend a few days with them in Cornwall. We had a lovely time together, walked miles along the coast, ate out, played Scrabble and Monopoly, laughed a lot and it was as though Sarah had always been in our lives. Even so, and as much as we had become very fond of her, we were somewhat taken aback when Peter phoned at the beginning of May to tell us that he had 'popped the question' and that they were getting engaged. He had known her for just six weeks.

'I'm the luckiest man alive, Mum,' he said. 'We're going to have an engagement party in October and you'll be able to meet Sarah's parents. Mike and Zoe can come up from Cornwall. There'll be loads of friends coming.' He went on again about how lucky he was.

As happy as the two of them were together, we felt things were moving along just a bit too quickly. All we could do was bite our tongues and let fate play its cards, but it was a call from Peter just a few days later, that began to sow, for John and I, real seeds of concern.

'But don't you think you ought to wait just a bit longer Peter?' I heard John say. 'Your flat is quite adequate for the time being.' There was more. He listened on again, frowning.

'Yes I know. But I do think you should think this through very carefully. What does Sarah think?'

Peter clearly had much to say as he talked on for some time. John eventually said 'I'll think about it and get back to you, but I think you are being too hasty.' Then, not best pleased, he slammed the phone down.

I made us a pot of coffee and we sat down at the kitchen table. John sighed. 'Peter wants to sell the flat and take out a mortgage on a house. They want to live together. He says he can run Sarah to the station in the mornings, she's quite happy to commute.'

I poured us a coffee whilst digesting all that John had said.

'I can understand them wanting to live together John, but he has a nice flat, big enough for two.'

'I know. But that's not all. He wants me to loan him the deposit. He just isn't thinking straight, but he's made up his mind.'

We sat quietly sipping our coffee, each wrestling with our conscience, pondering over this new problem.

Peter had never been particularly good at saving money and we were aware that there had been times when he had only just managed to keep his head above water. He had always lived life on the fast track and even more so since he had met Sarah, although they were both earning good wages and as far as we knew, pooled their resources. Perhaps we were being over-cautious.

From then on Peter began to phone us daily, anxious for John's decision. He had always valued his father's advice but on this issue he simply wouldn't listen to reason. He was utterly convinced that they could manage. After two weeks of wearisome calls we decided to give Peter the benefit of the doubt and he got his deposit.

At the beginning of September Peter and Sarah moved into a whitewashed Victorian terraced house not far from Brighton station. Perhaps wanting to prove a point and ease our minds, they invited us to stay just a few weeks later, for a long weekend. We decided to accept their invitation, thinking that if we saw their new home it might just allay our fears over Peter's impatience.

We were pleasantly surprised. For although much of the house needed decorating and upgrading, it certainly had potential and although DIY had never been a forte of Peter's, he was keen to begin and to learn.

With Sarah's books, belongings and feminine touches and with the beginnings of a lick of paint here and there, despite the place being sparsely furnished, they had managed to turn it into a comfortable home and were very proud of all they had achieved.

Sarah was coping with commuting to London and although admitting to feeling tired by the end of the week, she was managing to continue her studies.

We had never seen Peter so happy, animated and

Coming to Terms

talkative. He was in seventh Heaven, totally optimistic about anything and everything. He had agreed to pay back the deposit to John in installments and gave him the first cheque just before we left.

The engagement party in October was a great success. Their house was heaving with friends. Mike and Zoe came up from Cornwall and it was good to have the family together again. We were pleased to meet Sarah's mother and father who had travelled down from Oxfordshire.

The four of us had booked in at the same hotel, agreeing beforehand that it would give us a better opportunity to get to know one another. They told us that they too felt that Peter and Sarah's relationship had moved on at an alarming rate, especially as Sarah still had a huge amount of studying ahead of her.

But we all agreed that so far things were going well and most importantly, they were very happy

Towards the end of the evening of the party, I slipped out into the garden, feeling the need for some fresh air. Moments later Peter spotted me from the kitchen window and came out to join me.

'Hello Mum' he said as he put his arms around me.

'I just want you to know how happy I am. Are you pleased and happy for me?'

'What do you think Peter?' I said. 'Of course I am.'

A month later he was made redundant.

CHAPTER 5

November 1993 – July 1994

Over the following worrying days and restless nights we hardly dare answer the telephone. We still had at the back of our minds his breakdown of the previous year and we were concerned about what this new stressful situation might do to Peter. Two weeks later he phoned.

'Hi Mum. It's me. I'm ringing to tell you not to worry. I'm OK.'

'That's good' I said. 'But are you sure? We have been very concerned about you both.'

'I have been looking and I don't think I'll have too much trouble getting another job. I've got plenty of contacts with printing companies here. We'll be all right.'

'It was such a shock you see, Peter. But we'll keep our fingers crossed. Do let us know as soon as you have news.'

'Of course I will, Mum' and before I had chance to say another word he rang off. It had been thoughtful of him to phone, but even so I detected a hint of bravado in his voice.

We somehow managed to put it all to the back of our minds and get through Christmas. John and I spent it with my mother and my family in Norwich. Peter and Sarah went up to her parents in Oxford. They had been engaged for just over seven weeks.

But Peter had been right. By the second week in January he started work with another printing company and all appeared to be going well once more.

Coming to Terms

In the Spring, John and I went down to see Mike and Zoe. They were living at that time in a tiny, rented cottage in Penzance, not far from St. Michael's Mount. They worked together in a shop on the sea-front selling wooden games and novelties that Mike made, and a variety of juggling equipment, a skill they had mastered so that they could demonstrate to potential buyers. They were poor but happy and such a good team that a visit to them was always a tonic, even though we had to adapt to their Bohemian way of life for our stay with them.

We began to dare to relax and believe that all was well with our family until, a month after our return from Cornwall, Michael phoned us one evening and after giving me an update on all they had been doing he then said 'I'm worried about Peter, Mum.'

'Are you? Why's that Mike?'

'Well, he's just phoned to tell me he's thinking of buying Sarah a car. Surely he can't afford it. It's a crazy idea.'

'He certainly can't. What did you say?'

'I said he should look at his money a bit more carefully, they still have a lot to do on the house'.

'And what did he say to that?'

'Not much really. He just went quiet at first. I think he thought I'd encourage him and was disappointed. He just said I suppose you're right and then hung up on me.'

'But Dad and I have been thinking they were doing all right.'

'Perhaps they are, but he's living at such a pace and is so besotted with Sarah I think he just wants to impress her all the time. From what he keeps telling me he's spending money as though there's no tomorrow.'

I thanked Mike for phoning and felt a sense of foreboding as I told John that evening all that Mike had said. We all knew that Peter could be impulsive, but it had never been over anything serious. This time it mattered. We were thankful that Mike had been so sensible. Peter had occasionally sought his advice over the years. More often than not Mike's views were entirely in line with ours.

At that time, Peter was still in touch but not quite so regularly. We had no problem with that, knowing he had a new life with Sarah. He never ever mentioned the car.

At the beginning of July, we were delighted to have a call from Peter asking if he and Sarah could come and stay with us for a long weekend.

When they arrived Peter was very quiet, perhaps we thought, tired after the drive. However, at dinner he was subdued. Sarah was doing most of the talking.

I suggested the next morning that Sarah and I go shopping in town and leave the men to their own devices. I enjoyed her young company greatly and shopping with her was rather a novelty to me, not having had a daughter of my own.

We arrived home to a strained atmosphere.

Peter and John were sitting at the dining table, Peter with his chin in his hands looking on as John was carefully sifting through a pile of letters Peter had brought with him.

I made us all a cup of tea and Sarah suggested we join them, although Peter seemed reluctant for us to do so.

We were soon to understand why. The letters were unpaid bills, final demands to the tune of hundreds of pounds, and so our fears over Peter's inability to manage his financial affairs were fully realised as we sat at our table that day.

Sarah looked across at Peter in a state of incredulous disbelief.

'Why Peter? Why didn't you tell me? You said you were managing the money and were all right.' He shrugged his shoulders. 'I thought it would sort itself out. I didn't want to worry you.'

There was a long silence.

'But I thought we had no secrets.'

Tears began to stream down Sarah's face. I handed her a tissue and as I did so I thought about Mike's phone call about the car Peter had said he wanted to buy her. The idea had been so completely irrational and with the redundancy just a few months previously, his life was becoming more and more unstable. There was more.

Sarah wiped her eyes, then, not looking away from Peter said 'I might as well tell you. Peter has not been well. He is on antidepressants'.

There was another long pause as she waited for our reaction. Peter sat looking out of the window. John sat back and sighed. I felt sorry for him. He was under a huge amount of pressure at work at that time. He didn't need this. Eventually Peter broke the silence, perhaps feeling he must redeem himself in some way.

'I'm still managing to work' he said.

John and I looked at one another, wondering whether Peter had told Sarah about his breakdown of the previous year.

My heart bled for Sarah as she sat twisting and untwisting the tissue in her hand, her eyes still not leaving his face, willing him to look at her.

They had been together for less than a year and already her love was being tried and tested. Despite this it was clear she was still very devoted to him.

Slowly Sarah told us that Peter had been unwell for a month. He had been to their GP and had been taking antidepressants for just over two weeks. He still felt very low but thought that they were beginning to work. The doctor had told him he must be patient. By then I had bitten my tongue for long enough. I had to ease his mind.

'Dad and I will settle these bills for you, Peter. But you really must start to think very carefully about your spending.'

He slowly nodded, watching John who was gathering up the bills in front of him.

'Your mother is right, Peter. I want you to promise that from now on you and Sarah will look through your bills and come to a consistent arrangement together about paying them.

'I promise' said Peter.

'We will, and thank you' said Sarah.

The rest of the weekend was not easy, Peter overwhelming us with gratitude and trying his best to look relaxed and cheerful but struggling to do so. Sarah gradually recovered from the shock she had had and made the best of their time with us.

I was not totally convinced that Peter's breakdown was just about the money. I began to feel that there was something much deeper. The following day we drove them over to Haworth, looked round the parsonage and church and browsed in the shops in the steep main street there. There was a candy shop with a wonderful display of home-made sweets.   John suggested he treat us all to a bag of whatever we would like. Sarah, John and I had no problem choosing from the mouth-watering selection, but as they were being weighed, I noticed that Peter was having serious difficulty trying to make a decision as to which he would like and was becoming agitated. I went over to him and suggested that he could have a mixture in a bag, but even that was too much for him. He looked at me and shaking his head and frowning, walked out of the shop.

I followed him, and then linked my arm through his. John and Sarah followed on behind.

'Never mind' I said. 'You can have some of mine.'

'It's not that, Mum' he said.

'What do you mean Peter? What's the matter?'

'I just couldn't do it; I just couldn't make a decision.'

As we walked slowly back up the high street, his head was down as though he was studying the cobbles. I suddenly realised why he was so concerned and I suddenly felt cold.

The last time he had spoken very similar words to me was when he had tried to get on the train less than two years previously.

History was repeating itself.

CHAPTER 6

July 1994 –May 1995

Once again over the next three months, Peter slowly recovered and it said much for his inner strength that he managed to keep working. Sarah was a tremendous support and helped him through. They led a less hectic social life as Sarah was studying hard and they spent a lot of their time working and decorating their house which for Peter had been a therapy in itself. We were invited down to see them again in the autumn.

They made us feel very welcome and were keen to show us the results of their efforts. They had obviously worked very hard.

All seemed to be reasonably well and they had settled into a happy routine, although I noticed that Peter had become even quieter and I was troubled. He had developed a habit of staring ahead in a world of his own from time to time, stroking his chin with the palm of his right hand, as a man does who is feeling his unshaven stubble, turning his hand from right to left. The habit seemed to be too frequent to be normal. Although I tried to convince myself I was over-reacting, after our stay with them I was far from confident that Peter was totally at ease with himself; he had changed radically.

Michael's calls were always a tonic. This was particularly true of one he made to us in November of that year.

'Hi Mum. It's me. Are you sitting comfortably?'

'Hello Mike. Good to hear from you. Now why should I be sitting comfortably?'

'Because I've got some great news. You're going to be a

Grandma.'

'Really Mike?' I said, trying to collect my thoughts, wishing with all my heart that he and Zoe lived nearer. 'That's wonderful news, Mike. Congratulations.'

'Better get your knitting needles out Mum.'

'I certainly will; and how's Zoe? I'll bet she's thrilled to bits. Is she there?'

'No she's out at the moment but she wanted me to tell you and say she will phone you when she gets back. I might even get a proper job now, Mum'.

I laughed at that, for Michael's determination to work for no-one but himself was a family joke. We chatted on for a while before he rang off. Consumed with thoughts of his pending fatherhood, he hadn't a care in the world.
John was as delighted as me when he heard the news and we phoned to congratulate a very excited Zoe, who joked with us about Mike's comments on getting a proper job.

They decided to spend a quiet Christmas that year and we were pleasantly surprised when Peter phoned to say that he and Sarah would like to come up and spend Christmas with us.

'I am feeling tons better, Mum' he said.

'I feel as though I've a lot of catching up to do and I've got so much energy it's great. I've come off my tablets and the doctor has given me something to help me sleep, so you've to stop worrying about me.'

He was talking so enthusiastically to me that my mind went back to the time he phoned to tell us all about Sarah.

'You can come up whenever you like, Peter. It will be

lovely to see you both again.'

'OK, Mum' he said 'That's great. We'll drive up on Christmas Eve and stay until the day after Boxing Day.'

Before I had time to respond again he joked 'Better let Santa know we won't be in Brighton for Christmas,' then chuckling 'See you soon, Mum, love to Dad' and he put the phone down.

As I put my receiver down, I began to believe that he was finally well again. And as I cooked, shopped and prepared for their stay, I managed to put all my worries over him behind me.

The four of us had a lovely Christmas together, including a visit to the pantomime at the local theatre.

It was a wonderful production and we all, like the children and young families, hissed at the villain and cheered and sang, and for the first time in years we heard Peter laughing out loud.

As the year came to a close, with the baby to look forward to and with Peter and Sarah happily settled once more, it seemed that the family was having the boost we all so needed.

CHAPTER 7

May and June 1995

Jacob was born on May 23rd and as pre-arranged I travelled down by train to help for a few days when Zoe was discharged from hospital with the baby. John finished a business commitment and then drove down to Cornwall and joined me there.

What a joy it was to experience seeing our little Grandson for the first time!

Mike and Zoe were delighted with their little boy and he was indeed beautiful. We had such a nice time with them that John and I were determined that our trips down to Cornwall from then on would be much more regular, babysitting being high on the agenda.

Peter had always loved children and had been pleased at the news, but I sensed a forced enthusiasm when he phoned at that time. I made a decision to make another trip down to Brighton to ease my mind. Aware that I might be considered to be intruding, I made the excuse that I needed to catch up with friends, although Sarah sounded genuinely keen for me to go down again when I phoned to ask whether I could stay.

I travelled down to Brighton early in June.

Sarah welcomed me warmly on arrival, Peter much less so. He looked pale and tired, had lost weight and I knew at a glance that my instincts had been right. He carried my case up to the spare room, said 'I'm watching something on T.V.' then without as much as a smile went downstairs into their lounge. I unpacked, and going back downstairs on my way to the kitchen I looked round the lounge door. He was sitting staring at the TV screen at a programme that I knew wouldn't normally have appealed to him in the slightest. I felt hurt, for although he knew I was there, he didn't look up. He was deliberately ignoring me.

In the kitchen, Sarah was busy preparing the evening meal and declined my offer of help but poured me a glass of wine and suggested I sit at the kitchen table and talk to her. She then checked the food in the oven, turned the gas low under the saucepans, carefully closed the kitchen door and sat down facing me.

'I'm glad you've come, Arlene' she said 'I've something to tell you.'

'I think I can guess what it is, Sarah. It's Peter isn't it?'

'Yes, you're right. He is down again and is off work. The doctor has signed him off for a month and put him on some new anti-depressants.

'I see,' I said, my heart sinking. 'And do you think they're working, Sarah?'

'It's hard to tell really. Some days he's better than others.'

'How long has he been off work?'

'Two weeks.' She took a sip of wine and began slowly, absentmindedly, making faint lines on the tablecloth with a fork. Waiting for my response.

'What brought it about, do you think?'

'I think it was stress. He had been under a lot of pressure and finding it harder to cope and meet deadlines. It's odd really. He likes people as you know and gets on well with them. But a customer phoned Peter's boss and complained that Peter had been rude to him.'

Coming to Terms

Neither of us spoke as I studied the poor girl's face, not knowing what to say next and feeling totally inadequate. She got up and checked the meal.

'I feel as though Peter doesn't want me here, Sarah. Perhaps I shouldn't have come to stay with you.'

'No, please don't worry. He's got to take his misery out on someone I suppose.' She managed a smile, trying to make light of what she was going through.

'Look Sarah, I want you to remember that if you need backup support John and I are here for you. We don't want to interfere but this is hard for you.'

'I know. And I will' she said, forcing another smile.

Sarah and I laboured at conversation during the evening meal. Peter barely joined in and for much of the time only half listened. I helped Sarah clear away. Peter had muttered a 'Thanks, Sarah' and disappeared into the lounge again. I had another coffee with Sarah, showed her the latest photographs of Jacob I had brought with me, then made my excuses, thanked her and went up to bed, having decided that I would show them to Peter the next morning. I was best out of the way. Peter hadn't spoken more than a dozen words to me since I had arrived.

After an almost sleepless night I heard their alarm the next morning, then the shower, kitchen noises and hurried movement up and down the stairs, and finally the front door closing and their car engine starting.

Peter was running Sarah to the station.

I went downstairs, made myself a cup of tea and was sat warming my hands round it when I heard the key in the lock. Peter appeared at the kitchen door.

'I'm going back to bed' he said.

'Do you want a cup of tea Peter?' I ventured.

'No thanks' he said dismissively. 'I've just told you. I'm going back to bed.' And he was gone.

I sat for a very long time, my tea going cold, remembering the way he had looked at me. It was disturbing. I might as well have been a complete stranger. Their morning paper was pushed through the door and I tried to concentrate and read the latest news but couldn't. I made myself a piece of toast then showered and dressed and left the house.

I had made arrangements to meet a friend in town but it was still very early so I took myself for a long walk on the seafront, envying as I did so the people enjoying coffees in the various cafes there. Surely they had troubles too?

I bought myself a coffee and managed to make it last an age, sitting in a quiet corner of a café, watching the world go by outside. Killing time.

I later met my friend and was glad I had photographs of Jacob and could enthuse about our trip down to Cornwall. I lied about Peter and Sarah, fearing I would have lost control and not wanting to spoil our time together.

After we parted company I lingered again, shop-window gazing before making my way back via a supermarket. Sarah had welcomed my suggestion that I make the evening meal. Back at their house I rang their doorbell and after what seemed an eternity, Peter opened the door and silently stepped back to let me through into the hall. He was still in his dressing gown and it was 4pm. Again he declined my offer of a drink. I made myself a cup of tea and dared to join him in the lounge. There were two empty mugs on the coffee table and an apple core. The newspaper was strewn over the floor. I sipped my tea, occasionally glancing at him as he sat watching the endless TV. There he was again, stroking his chin. Right and left. Right and left. Realising it was futile to hope that he might talk to me, I went into the kitchen and began to prepare the meal. A while later I heard the front door slam and was thankful that Peter could at least manage to collect Sarah from the station.

Sarah seemed glad to see me and overwhelmed me with thanks for making the meal, although I felt that it was the very least I could do.

I stayed on for two more days but the time dragged, mainly because Peter was intent on ignoring me. I walked miles back and forth along the sea front, visited a couple of friends who made me feel welcome, and again prepared evening meals. I did what I could to help. Sarah was adamant that I wasn't interfering when I told her of Peter's attitude towards me, and insisted that she was pleased to have me there.
'Please don't worry' she had said. 'I'm learning to be tough. We'll be all right. I have some good friends here who are very supportive. I love my job, it fills my mind when I'm not here, and I am still managing to study. Peter will get better. We just have to be patient really.'

I admired her courage and positive attitude as I travelled home, wishing I had felt her confidence in Peter's recovery.

We were to see further examples of Sarah's efforts with Peter a month later.

We have a timeshare lodge in Scotland not far from the Balmoral Estate and spend a week there every year in September. The lodge, situated on a hill amongst pine trees, is just ten minutes walk from the River Dee. We spend our week there walking, biking, swimming in the nearby indoor pool and occasionally we go pony trekking or just spend our time reading and relaxing. We have some wonderful memories of family holidays there over the years.

A few weeks after my visit to Brighton, Sarah phoned one evening to say that she had persuaded Peter that it may be good for them to get away for a few days and that they would like to join us in Scotland.

We were delighted, and agreed that the change would be just what Peter needed. We were equally pleased when Mike phoned to say that he and Zoe would be coming too so that we could catch up on Jacob.

Peter and Sarah drove up to us the night before we were due to travel to Scotland and stayed overnight. Peter looked much worse than when I had last seen him and Sarah looked utterly weary, but, stoic as ever, she enthused about the forthcoming holiday, having never been to Scotland. Her lively chatter, although obviously forced at times, helped us through what would have been a very difficult evening. Peter spoke to us only when spoken to and John and I decided to leave him to it, hoping against hope that the holiday might just make a difference.

Peter and Sarah followed us up to Scotland in their car the next day. Mike and Zoe flew up to Aberdeen from Bristol and John drove across and picked them up at the airport.

We were pleased to see Mike and Zoe again, and Jacob, having not seen them since his birth in May. He had grown into a most beautiful and engaging child, so contented that he was forever smiling and chuckling. It was a treat just to watch and enjoy him.

Mike and Zoe did well disguising their shock at seeing the change in Peter, and it was thanks to their sterling efforts and determination that we would enjoy ourselves that we managed to have a reasonably good holiday. Peter joined in various activities, although afterwards he was exhausted out of all proportion to what he had been doing. We would encourage him to come on walks we had always enjoyed together over the years but he showed no interest at all. On one occasion he started out on a walk with Sarah but they came back to the lodge after an hour as he had told her he was far too tired. We all felt sorry for Sarah who tried her best, but it became patently clear that she was getting nowhere.

If Peter was to show any interest in anything at all it was in his little nephew, who without a doubt was a ray of sunshine throughout the week. The only time Peter seemed to be and look contented, was when he was sitting with Jacob on his knee.

We were sorry when the week came to an end as it had been such a treat to be in Mike and Zoe's lively company, although our sadness at parting was coupled with a growing anxiety over Peter and Sarah's future. It was patently clear that Sarah's theory that the week's holiday would make a difference to Peter had failed miserably.

CHAPTER 8

October 1995

A month later there was no change in Peter. Sarah's optimism slowly faded and our anxieties grew as she began to phone us from work, expressing her concerns.

Peter had started drinking heavily. She had had to resort to hiding money from him when she went to work or she would find him in a drunken stupor when she got home. He was still driving her to the station in the mornings, but she had taken to walking home at night. Coping with him was beginning to affect her studies.

Peter had been off work for three months at that time, and his medication was making not the slightest difference.

Convinced by then that there was something radically wrong with Peter, the thought that he might take his life played on our minds more, until, beginning to clutch at straws, we decided that Peter should see a psychiatrist.

Waiting weeks or possibly months for an appointment was out of the question. Sarah readily agreed with us and I phoned their GP and arranged for a referral letter. We would pay for a private appointment. Peter saw the specialist a week later, then two weeks after that.

Yet again, any glimmer of hope faded as after two visits to the specialist Peter had begun to say to Sarah 'I don't like him.' Simply 'I don't like him.' But he would never say why.

By then, Peter had become my waking and sleeping thought. Worries about him consumed me, as I began to lose interest in all that my busy life normally involved. I had to force myself to eat, as I lost my appetite and was losing weight. I began borrowing books from the library on depression. I became easily tearful and even began to wonder whether I was slipping into a depression too. Unable to bear it any longer, and desperate to see if there was any more I could do to help Sarah, I decided to go down to Brighton again, this time to talk to Peter's specialist. I made an appointment. I had to know more. Even though Peter's behaviour was irrational and angry at that time, we had to know why he didn't like the man. There had to be a reason why, something deeper. By then we knew without a doubt that Peter needed serious help, and we were convinced that he knew it too.

I travelled down, again by train. John had a meeting in London and suggested that he would drive down on the Friday evening and we could then drive back together on the Sunday. I was glad I had braced myself as I rang their doorbell, for what a pitiful sight the two young people were as I walked through the front door. Weariness was written all over their faces. Peter was unshaven; his hair was in need of a wash. His eyes looked deep and sunken as I had seen them once before, and he had lost more weight. He was standing leaning against the banister with his arms folded. The look he gave me was so cold it frightened me.

Sarah looked tired and cried as I hugged her. I turned to Peter again to say 'Hello' but he continued to look at me coldly. I was no longer welcome in his home.

Jaw set, he looked at Sarah, then again at me, and then walked past us both and into the lounge, closing the door behind him. The atmosphere in the house was chilly.

Sarah looked at me and shook her head.

She must have registered the look of shock in my face. 'Don't worry' she said, picking up my case. 'I'll take this up for you, and then we'll have a cup of tea.'

Minutes later, we were sat again as on my previous visit, facing each other at the kitchen table. This time it was to be very different. This time I felt a strong sense of foreboding as I waited to hear what Sarah had to say. Words I had been expecting and had dreaded hearing for a very long time.

'I'm sorry Arlene, but I'm breaking the engagement. I can't take any more. I'm going to look for a flat back in London and move out.'

She sounded so matter of fact; it was as though she had been rehearsing what she was going to say to me. She then sat looking at me, waiting. All I felt was an overwhelming pity for this lovely young woman who had stolen Peter's heart and once loved him so dearly. She had given him her all for two years but had had no life with him for a very long time.

'Have you told Peter?' I said gently.

'No, not yet. I've been waiting until you were here.' She began to lose her composure.

'I've been so worried. I don't know what he'll do. I feel so guilty.' Tears began to fall down her pretty face.

It was with a very heavy heart that I watched her weep and I fought back tears of my own, as I considered the gravity of this new and yet not unexpected situation.

'Please don't worry. You have been wonderful' I said gently. 'There is nothing to feel guilty about. You have had a very hard time and John and I will always be grateful to you for all you have done. We'll look after Peter. You know that.'

She sat and slowly nodded in response.

Coming to Terms

'I thought you'd be disappointed in me.'

I fumbled for a tissue in my bag and handed it to her.

'Not at all, we'll be sorry to lose you.' She wiped her eyes and then sat gazing out of the window, lost in thought, before saying quietly to herself, her decision made, 'I'll tell Peter in the morning.'

As on my previous visit, Sarah and I laboured at conversation during the evening meal. Peter didn't say a word, but just moved his food round his plate until he finally pushed his plate away, stood up and, almost knocking his chair over as he did so, left the table and walked out of the room.

Sarah slowly put down her knife and fork and I did the same. Neither of us had an appetite.

The following morning I made my way to the clinic to see the psychiatrist. It was a warm, sunny morning and I had decided to walk, passing as I did so many familiar landmarks I knew so well, from the time we had lived happily down in Brighton without the dark cloud that was now hovering over our lives. I felt uneasy about meeting Dr Darwood for fear of what he might say, wondering whether Peter's illness was irreversible and if so, wondering how I might react.

The clinic was easy to find and was situated on a wide road that ran parallel to the seafront. Gulls screamed overhead as I walked down the drive and through the huge front door of the large bay-windowed detached house that had once been a family home. A receptionist was sitting at a desk in the corner of the dark, panelled hall, busily typing. After checking my name she directed me up the stairs to the landing where leading off were the various bedrooms now used as consulting rooms for the 4 consultants.

I sat down in the waiting area facing a sad-looking young woman who gave me an expressionless, vague nod. I smiled at her but then forced myself to look away, as I noticed she had a habit of twisting and turning her hands in her lap as though she couldn't ever stop. I hadn't been waiting long before a door opened and a grey-suited young woman appeared from one of the rooms. 'Mrs. Hindle?' she said solemnly.

'Will you follow me, please?' I did so, and she led me to a room at the far end of the landing and at the back of the house.

'Dr Darwood' she said, before turning, her heels clicking on the wooden floor as she walked away.

Dr Darwood was sitting, almost silhouetted, his back to the window, behind an enormous desk piled high with papers and patients' notes. He stood up as I entered, walked round his desk and shook hands with me, then without a word indicated that I should take a seat. I watched his face as he carefully turned the pages of the notes in front of him, trying to see him with Peter's eyes. He was of medium height and slightly built with a head of thinning, grey hair. His wire-framed glasses did nothing to redeem his sharp featured face. As an anxious mother I would have welcomed an understanding smile, but instead waited, listening to my heart pounding for what seemed an eternity before he closed the file in front of him and looked at me over his glasses.

I took a deep breath and then said 'I have come to see you because my husband and I are very seriously concerned about Peter. He is not getting any better and this has gone on for far too long.'
'I know' he said. He paused, then in a very matter of fact tone said, 'I have told him that unless he gets a job he will be unemployable for the rest of his life.'

Coming to Terms

My jaw must have dropped, for I was momentarily stunned, unable to take in what I had just heard.

'But he is in a terrible state. He can't make a decision. He couldn't possibly work as he is, he is so depressed.' There was another long pause as he continued looking at me over his glasses, waiting for me to speak again. I began to feel thoroughly uncomfortable.

I tried again.

'Are you aware that his uncle committed suicide?'

Raising his eyebrows he said,

'Oh, I know that,' speaking in a tone that suggested I had no right to imply that he had no knowledge of it. My heart sank. I was getting nowhere.

Had this so called 'specialist' really not noticed how ill our son was?

I thought of Peter, sitting as I was, in front of this man who I had already decided I didn't like either. Exasperated I tried, 'But his fiancée is breaking their engagement. She can't live with him any longer as he is.'

Again those raised eyebrows. 'I'm not surprised,' he said.

I began to feel as though this was some kind of nightmare. Had this man not taken in all that must have been written in the notes in front of him? Almost three years of Peter's life lost to misery and breakdowns. There just had to be a reason for it all. Was it really necessary for me to spell out all Peter had been through? I decided there and then that Dr Darwood's attitude was so indifferent I would be wasting my breath. Instead I said 'If you feel you can't help Peter we are going to take him home with us. He is in no fit state to live alone.'

He looked me hard in the face over his glasses again. 'Do what you feel you must, but you'll have to watch him very carefully if you do.'

I couldn't believe my ears. Now he was being contradictory, on the one hand implying that Peter was capable of pulling himself together and on the other suggesting that he needed watching. I decided that a further attempt on Peter's behalf would be pointless. Nor was I prepared to risk being humiliated even further. Dr Darwood had simply nothing to offer.

Feeling bitter disappointment and also angry after all I had been subjected to, I resolved that Peter would never, ever set eyes on Dr Darwood again. Then, concluding that this insensitive man didn't deserve the courtesy of a 'thank you' I got up, turned on my heels, and without another word, walked out.

But my visit hadn't been a complete waste of time. For I had learned in much less then 5 minutes why Peter didn't like Dr Darwood.

It was because he was wrong.
I made my way through the back streets, not wanting to be seen as I cried tears of frustration, guilt too, as I thought of Peter being subjected to such an unprofessional attitude.

I arrived back at the house and went straight in to Peter who was still in his dressing gown in the middle of the day, sitting staring at the screen. I sat down beside him. 'I'm sorry about Dr Darwood, Peter.' I said 'I didn't like him either.'

He shrugged. 'No one listens to me. You all think I'm lazy and not bothering.'

He began stroking his chin.

Coming to Terms

'You know that's not true, Peter, we all want to help you.' He shrugged again, turned his head away and began staring out of the window.

'I wish you would talk to me. I miss you' I said, feeling a lump in my throat.

It was as though he hadn't heard. He didn't respond. I longed to put my arms round him and take away his pain and waited, hoping he might say something more. Anything. But there was nothing and I was treading on glass.

'If it's any consolation to you Peter, you'll not have to see Dr Darwood again, I'll make sure of it. We'll find a way to get you well again. I promise'.

I was relieved to see John when he arrived that evening, although he was visibly upset when Peter gave him the same cool reception he had given me.

I let him settle in after his busy day in London before telling him about my interview with Doctor Darwood. He was furious that I had been subjected to such rudeness and disappointed that Peter's appointments with him had been so fruitless. Hearing that Sarah was to break the engagement was the final straw, but like me he wasn't in the least surprised and managed to find a few moments on his own with her in the garden to tell her so, and thank her for all she had done.

We somehow struggled through that evening. John worked hard at trying to lift the atmosphere as each of us picked away at the meal. Peter eventually pushed his plate of untouched food away, and without a word got up and walked out, leaving the three of us in silent mutual understanding before leaving the table ourselves.

John and I barely slept that night, having talked over what

more we could do for Peter. Fearful of his reaction to the broken engagement, we could see no alternative other than taking him home with us. Leaving him to live on his own after Sarah had moved out was unthinkable. We would have to live with his hostility until he was better; neither of us doubted for a moment that somehow we would get him through.

The following morning after breakfast, Sarah made two cups of coffee then glanced at us, anguish written all over her face, before taking them into the front room, where Peter had been sitting as ever staring at the T.V. We heard her close the door then moments later the T.V. was silenced, as Peter was to hear that his future with her was not to be.

I busied myself in the kitchen clearing up then started on a pile of ironing. Anything, other than just sitting and waiting as Peter's world was falling apart in the next room.

John sat at the kitchen table scanning the morning paper, blindly turning the pages.

Some time later Sarah came back into the kitchen and, hearing Peter go out and slam the front door, John moved quickly to follow him. Sarah sat down at the table and dissolved into tears.

'I'll never, ever forget the look on his face when I told him. I feel terrible.'

I unplugged the iron, sat down beside her and put my arm round her.

'Don't punish yourself Sarah. You've had a very hard time. No one is blaming you. I think your Mum and Dad will be relieved. They will have been worrying no end about you.'

'They have. But I felt so sure I could go on coping.'

Coming to Terms

'You'll feel better soon and you know that John and I will look after Peter.' I waited a few more moments until she appeared calmer.

'We're going to take him home with us tomorrow. Perhaps it will help if we take him away from Brighton for a while.'

'Perhaps' she said, wiping her eyes.

I took courage. 'Now I'd like to take you out for lunch. I think we both need cheering up, don't you? John will stay here with Peter.'

And so Sarah and I went out and made the most of what we both knew would probably be the last day we would ever spend together.

Later that night, I was to hear from John that he had followed Peter to a local park where he found him sitting with his head in his hands, utterly desolate. We knew that he wouldn't want to come back home with us and he had argued bitterly with John when the suggestion was put to him.

Peter's denial that Sarah no longer loved or wanted him was so acute that he still believed he could stay with her. The shock of losing her was so terrible, he was far beyond any clear thinking as he cried. John gently asked him to suggest what else he could do, where else he could go, but Peter had nothing to offer, and sadly, nor had we.

The following morning, Peter wandered around the house like a lost child as Sarah and I packed his clothes and other belongings that he might possibly, in time, appreciate having with him.

Sarah wasn't looking forward to being on her own, but reassured us that we were not to worry about her as she would soon find accommodation in London. She had phoned her parents with her news and they would go down and see her in a couple of day's time. Already she had begun to think positively and was looking forward to concentrating fully on her studies.

Even so, it was heart-wrenching seeing their sad faces as she and Peter hugged one another and said their goodbyes at the door. Peter then, slowly shaking his head, walked to our car and before opening the door, turned and gave Sarah a look that spoke volumes.

We drove home in silence, John and I knowing only too well that attempts at conversation would be futile. We stopped for a light meal on the way, Peter wordlessly pointing to an item he wanted on the menu, which he then quickly ate before getting up and walking out where he stood leaning on the car, arms folded waiting for us. Angry. His jaw set.

We were taking him away from Sarah and he was making it clear that what we were doing was unforgivable. John and I were learning fast how testing and difficult the days ahead would be. But no matter how badly Peter was behaving, he was very ill. We had to remember that.

Never had we been so glad to get home. Peter snatched his holdall from John and walked through the house straight to the spare room; he refused food and didn't reappear for the rest of the evening. It was hard to take, but so were the following weeks, as Peter further deteriorated.

CHAPTER 9

November 1995

'I am thirty two years old and living with my Mum and Dad.'

Words we were to hear Peter mutter to himself again and again. It was as though he hated himself as well as us for all that his life had become. Suffering terribly over his broken engagement and missing Sarah desperately, he would dismiss anything we said in our attempts at comforting him.

'It's your fault. You've dragged me away from her. You should have left us alone.'

In his denial and longing for her he blamed us entirely. In the space of just a few days our lives became a nightmare as we faced up to his hostility, as well as the reality of how very ill he was.

The morning after we brought Peter home, I managed to make him an urgent appointment with our GP, Dr Briar, and fortunately had no difficulty in persuading Peter to see him. He had remembered Dr Briar from when he was with us after his earlier breakdown. The doctor recommended a relatively new antidepressant and Peter was to take one a day in the mornings and see him again in three weeks' time.

Peter would sleep very late and refuse breakfast. I learned eventually to leave him alone. He would clumsily make himself a mug of coffee, often spilling the milk everywhere, then sit on the back doorstep always for an age, staring ahead, stroking his chin. Back and forth. Back and forth. I began to watch for him to do so. Sometimes it would be well into the afternoon before he made any attempt at showering and getting dressed. Meals were very much a hit and miss affair. Some days he would eat, others he would pick away at his food then push his plate away as we had seen him do so many times before. Occasionally he would take himself off for a walk and I would watch the clock, never comfortable until he arrived back at the house, when he would either shut himself in his room or sit as so often before, staring at the TV.

There were times when I felt like smashing the screen.

John was under huge pressure with his job at that time and was working long days as well as occasionally having commitments that meant that he was away for two or three days at a time. He worried about me as well as Peter and would leave him small undemanding projects to do in his office, in an attempt at some kind of therapy and to fill Peter's days.

Peter would grudgingly begin, but his concentration levels were so limited that within an hour he would give up, using the excuse that it was boring. There were times when life became an emotional see-saw, for right out of the blue Peter would smile at me and say 'Can I talk to you Mum?' He would then pour out all that was in his heart and his mind, for what sometimes would be hours. I became adept at stopping anything I was doing and would sit listening to him, but learned also not to voice an opinion, for if I did so I would be told 'You don't know what it's like' and he would storm away and I would lose him again. Until the next time. Once in a while he would ask me to walk with him and I was glad to be asked, for I hated him leaving the house on his own. He would rarely speak on those walks. He just seemed to want me to be there.

Thoughts of John's brother never far from my mind, I never, ever left Peter alone in the house. He never knew it but I even began following him at a short distance when he went on his walks, so concerned was I that he might not come back, or that he might do something foolish.

Coming to Terms

It was during the first two weeks that Peter was with us that his cousin Jonathan, who lived in Skipton, and had a stationery business, phoned and asked if Peter would like to work for him for just a few hours each week. He knew of Peter's background in the printing industry and felt that his offer might appeal, as well as being of some help.

'No thanks' Peter had said; 'I'm not working for family.' That was it, and despite our pleas that just an hour or so now and again might occupy his mind, he was adamant. We despaired.

Thoughts of Sarah continued to haunt Peter as he struggled to come to terms with losing her. He imagined in his ill and irrational mind that she was sleeping with other men, and such thoughts absolutely tortured him. I tried time and time again to convince him that this just wouldn't be the case but he was completely beyond reasoning. About three weeks after he had been with us, he phoned to talk to her. She was kind to him but in no way did she respond to his pleading. Instead, unwittingly adding salt to his wound, she told him that she had found somewhere else to live and would be moving out in the next few days. Peter was devastated, and we stood by helplessly as he wept.

As well as having to cope with Peter at that time, there was also the problem of the house in Brighton to consider. Peter and Sarah had been paying the mortgage jointly when they were together and the house was in Peter's name. When Sarah moved out, when and if Peter recovered from his depression, there was no way he would be able to afford to live there again. Cruel though it seemed to be at that time, we had no choice but to put the house on the market. We told Peter what we had decided to do but by then he had lost all interest in the house, which in its way was a blessing. Fortunately a good friend of John's was an estate agent and, learning of our problem, he reassured us that he would deal with the sale for us and keep in regular touch.

It was hard, having to think about practicalities at such an emotionally charged time, and the jolt about the house acted as a reminder to us also that Peter's car was still in Brighton. It was when John phoned Sarah to let her know that the house was to be put on the market that the problem began to resolve itself, although in a way we would not have chosen. Sarah suggested driving the car to Birmingham where she had friends she could stay with overnight, before travelling back to Brighton by train. Peter could meet her in Birmingham then drive his car back to Harrogate. It was a sensible suggestion, but she was totally unaware of just how much further Peter had deteriorated since their separation, and the repercussions her suggestion might cause. When John suggested to Peter that he wasn't well enough to drive so far and that he would collect the car instead, he was furious and no way would he be persuaded that it was the right thing to do.

'I might get her back if I go myself' he said.

'And you're not going to stop me.'

He was so adamant that we had no choice but to let him do as he wished.

Peter travelled to Birmingham the following weekend. Thoughts of his safety as a driver in his present state were at the forefront of our minds as we watched the clock that day and awaited his safe arrival home. When he finally walked through the door, he looked absolutely shattered, went straight to his room without a word and didn't reappear until the next morning.

Peter never told us what had been said when he met Sarah that day and we didn't ask. But seeing her again had set the final seal on their break-up for him and fate had played its cards. For no matter how hard it must have been for him, he never mentioned her name to us again.

Michael would phone every few days and talk to Peter. He was so concerned about him. Then he suggested that it might help if Peter was to go down and stay with him and Zoe. He felt that it would help John and I if we had a break too. But Jacob was then only six months old and Peter's moods and behaviour were so hard to cope with at that time that sensibly we all finally agreed that he was best staying with us. We suggested that once he began to show signs of recovery he could go down and stay with them in Cornwall as he had done after his first breakdown.

We watched for just a glimmer of a sign that Peter's tablets were beginning to take effect, but there were none. Just to be sure he was taking them conscientiously, when he was out of the way I would count them carefully each day. In doing so I brought about a change of events that I have often pondered since might have been very different indeed.

Late one Saturday morning, just three weeks after Peter had come to stay, John, with much difficulty, managed to persuade Peter to go for a walk with him for half an hour before lunch. What luxury it was to have time to myself. I prepared a salad lunch, set the table then went to Peter's bedroom to count his tablets. Then counted them again. Peter had taken nine tablets since I had counted them the previous morning.

Nine.

He might just as well have taken a hundred, such was my shock and fear. He had overdosed.

My heart racing, I phoned and asked to speak to our GP. I had no idea where John and Peter had gone for their walk, but I was thankful that Peter was not alone, that they wouldn't be far away, and looking up at the kitchen clock, anticipated that they would be home within the next few minutes.

Dr Briar was very kind and although unable to reassure me that I had no need to be worried, said calmly 'I want you to phone me as soon as Peter and John get back. I need to come and see him.' The next ten minutes were the longest of my life as my imagination took flight. I visualised Peter collapsed, and a confused John leaving him, running to get help.

I almost wept with relief when the two of them walked through the door.

Explaining briefly to John why I was doing so, I phoned the surgery. Peter listened then sat down at the table.

'You should stop interfering and leave me alone. I can look after myself' was all he had to say.

The three of us waited in silence, John and I watching the clock, too anxious to speak as we waited for the doorbell to ring.

Eventually Dr Briar arrived and followed me into the kitchen, pulled out a chair and sat facing Peter across the table. He spoke to him very gently and quietly.

'I'm afraid you are going to have to be admitted to hospital, Peter.'

'Why?' he asked indignantly.

'Because your mother has told me that you have taken more tablets than you should have done.'

John and I exchanged a glance. The doctor hadn't used the word 'overdose' and we were curious.

Coming to Terms

But we were to learn.

'Why did you take so many tablets at once, Peter?'

He didn't speak for an age. We waited and waited. Our eyes focused on his weary, miserable face.

'I thought I would get better quicker.'

Again John and I looked at one another, both of us relieved. Peter hadn't wanted to take his life and we had been living in fear of it. He wanted to get better. Perhaps this was a start after all.

'Why do I have to go into hospital?' Peter then said to the doctor.

'Because unfortunately your tablets can have serious side effects and you need to be under observation for the next 24 hours.'

Peter looked at John and I and smiled. We knew precisely why.

For it was a triumphant smile. He had found an escape route from us. At last.

John and I drove Peter to the hospital and on the way there he amazed us by saying 'It will do you both good to have time to yourselves.'

Clutching at straws as we had so often done by then, it was another small comfort. An indication that despite all he had put us through, Peter had recognised how difficult our lives had become. Arriving at the hospital we checked in and were directed to the men's medical ward. Peter smiled pleasantly at the nurse as she took down his details and was clearly enjoying the experience of being in another environment.

The nurse directed us to a bed in the corner of a six bedded ward. Peter sat on the bed and looked around him, pleased with himself, taking in his new surroundings. Then with a nod, acknowledged the patient, an elderly gentleman, in the bed opposite. He was behaving as though he had arrived on holiday. Within five minutes a doctor appeared, pulled the screen round the bed and introduced himself.

'Hello Peter, and this is your mother and father I take it.'

Peter nodded.

'I am going to examine you Peter, as you have to be carefully monitored. One of the side effects of the tablets you have taken is heart irregularity. We need to regulate your heartbeat. That is why you have been admitted.'

Peter expressed a polite 'Thank you.'

He looked across at us, willing us to leave. We had decided to go anyway.

We thanked the doctor and arranged to phone the following morning. Then, wishing Peter good luck, which he acknowledged with a confident 'I'll be OK', we left. Although we were thankful for a few hours to ourselves, we were not to have a restful night.

The next morning John phoned and we learned that Peter was physically fine, although he had been transferred to the psychiatric unit, which endorsed the fact that beyond his physical state, he was still far from well. His tablets were discontinued and an urgent appointment had been arranged for him to see a local psychiatrist, a Dr Lawson.

The following day John and I visited Peter on the psychiatric ward. A nurse directed us to the smoking room where Peter was sitting with a young man who was probably in his early twenties. He was sat in a corner smoking, was painfully thin and looked like death. The room reeked of stale smoke and the ash trays were piled high and spilling over with cigarette stubs. There were torn and discarded newspapers and magazines scattered on chairs and on the floor. It was an appalling and dismal room, but so many depressives smoke that we imagined that, awful as it was, the staff had to provide the facility for their patients who were addicted to the habit. Peter greeted us with a brief nod.

'This is Mark' he said, looking and smiling at the unfortunate young man, who by way of response just looked across at us then inhaled deeply on his cigarette.

'Sit down if you want' said Peter.

John and I did so. John said 'Are you feeling better, Peter?'

He shrugged. 'I wasn't feeling ill.'

Choosing his words carefully John then said 'We know, Peter. But you might have been. We had to let the doctor know. Surely you can see that.'

Peter shrugged again. Mark continued smoking, head down, staring at us.

'We've not come to stay Peter' I said. 'We've just come to see if there is anything you need. Mike sends his love.'

'Is he all right?' he said, vaguely interested.

Yes, he is. And says to tell you he'll phone you when you get home again.'

'Fine' Peter said. 'Say hello to him for me.'

'I will. It's a shame he is so far away.'

Peter nodded, and then began stroking his chin. John and I stood up and made to leave.

'Bye' said Peter curtly.

Smiling briefly at Mark, John and I walked out of the room and closed the door.

Glad to breathe in the cooler, fresh air as we walked out of the ward, we passed on our way a young woman who gave us such a piercing look it was disconcerting. She had long dark straggly hair and was dressed in a brightly striped hospital dressing gown that seemed to contradict her desolate image as she slowly walked passed us, muttering quietly to herself, her hands deep in her pockets.

A nurse was sitting reading by the door to a side ward where we noticed a woman asleep, her bed partially screened, but not to be let out of sight.

I wept as we drove home.

Whilst lying awake in the night, searching my mind for some way in which I could make Peter's stay with us more bearable for him, I hit upon the idea of making his room look more masculine. The following morning I removed the flowered covers from his bed and took down the curtains. I went into town and bought new fabric, in an abstract design, the main colour being blue. I removed delicate ornaments from a shelf in the corner of the room and replaced them with framed photographs of Peter and his brother in happier days. I hung a picture of Mike's on the wall at the foot of Peter's bed. The room was transformed.

Peter was discharged the following day and John brought him home.

'Do you like your new room?' I asked him. He shrugged his shoulders.

'I suppose so' he said. 'But I'm still with my Mum and Dad aren't I?'

I chose to ignore his last remark but felt that at least I had achieved something. I knew he wouldn't volunteer any enthusiasm.

Peter hated being back home with us. We had been wrong in thinking that the shock of hospitalisation would in some way make a difference. His behaviour was just as before, and I began to feel as though his depression was contagious, so miserable were my days too.

We began to pin our hopes on what Dr Lawson might say. Surely a second psychiatrist would succeed where Dr Darwood had so miserably failed.

The appointment was at a hospital in Ripon, some ten miles away from our home. Peter was furious because I insisted on going with him as John had a meeting. At first I offered to drive him there, for his behaviour had become so aggressive that again we didn't feel that he would drive safely. But after a terrible argument with John in which he said that he would refuse to go to the appointment unless he drove himself, we finally had to succumb.

He bitterly resented John's insistence that I should go with him but surprisingly, as though making a point, he drove to Ripon carefully, much to my relief.

The clinic was situated in a dark, grey stone building that had once been a school built in the Victorian era. The walls and high iron window frames of the outpatients' waiting room were painted in the same shade of cold pale green gloss paint, highlighted by the strip lighting on the much flaking ceiling. The walls were lined with racks and shelves jammed with countless leaflets and information on the many services available. There were piles of well-thumbed newspapers and magazines scattered on the few empty chairs and a side table.

A nurse would appear every so often, call out a name and an anxious patient would follow her to see the particular specialist they had been referred to. One of the nurses apologised because a session was running late. There were mumbling complaints from some who had no sense of recognising the pressures the nurses were under. I felt sorry for her.

Peter sat looking around him, taking it all in. Every so often he would pick up a magazine, flick through the pages and then almost throw it down again, mad with himself for not being able to concentrate. And there he was again, stroking his chin. I wondered what the specialist would make of the habit.

'Do you want me to come in with you, Peter?' I asked.

I so dearly hoped that he might, but he looked at me as though I had insulted him. Sitting further along the row from us was a boy in his late teens, head down, as though he had the world on his shoulders. His mother was talking quietly to him, worry written all over her face. He would snap at her or shrug his shoulders, not in the least interested in what she was saying. I longed to talk to her. I knew so exactly what she was going through.

Peter's name was eventually called and he got up and followed the nurse through a large door at the end of the corridor. The mother looked up at me after he had gone. Her sad face spoke realms.

After what had seemed an eternity and yet was only half an hour, Peter reappeared and, ignoring me, made for the exit. I struggled to keep up with him as he strode ahead, then waited impatiently for me to unlock the car doors before he got in and slammed his door.

Jaw set, and without saying a word to me, he concentrated on driving through the heavy traffic and out onto the outskirts of Ripon where to my horror, he began driving at high speed. I was terrified.

'Please slow down, Peter' I said. 'There's no need for this.'

He took no notice until, cursing and exasperated, he had to pull up sharply behind a large van. Hugely relieved and hoping it might calm his mood, I asked gently, 'How did you get on?

'I didn't. She said there's nothing wrong with me, I've just got a personality problem.'

'What?' I said incredulously

'I've just told you. She says I've got a personality problem. A disorder she said.'

'But that's crazy Peter.'

'Perhaps she thinks I am crazy really.'

'That's nonsense. You're having a rotten time.' He drove on, whilst I tried to make sense of what I had just heard. There was more.

Peter began again.

'She says I've got to get a job.'

I chose not to speak. A vision of Dr Darwood crossed my mind. He had said the same. Yet imagining Peter working in his present state was still beyond me. Surely two psychiatrists can't have been wrong. But they didn't live with him. They didn't see.

Peter tried to overtake the van a couple of times but on

each occasion had to brake sharply as there was oncoming traffic and each time I had to yell at him 'Don't Peter, please.' I sat with my fists tightly closed, hardly daring to look ahead.

The rest of the journey was a complete nightmare as he drove like a madman. Motorists were tooting their horns at him as he began overtaking, dangerously, time and time again, for the rest of the journey. Finally, he pulled in to the drive, turned off the engine but sat gripping the steering wheel.

I let out a long sigh of relief. Then said 'Perhaps you should take the specialist's advice and try and work, Peter. It will be hard for you but it might help. Perhaps the doctors are right.'

He waited a few seconds, perhaps pondering on what I had said. He then got out of the car and walked in front of me into the house, whereupon he went straight up to his room and slammed the door. As I had expected he didn't reappear at all for the remainder the day.

The following morning we were to have the surprise of our lives. Peter came into the kitchen much earlier than usual. Without as much as a glance at John and I who were sitting at the kitchen table finishing our breakfast, he made himself a coffee then took it into the hall. We watched him as he stood leaning on the desk sipping his coffee, looking out through the glazed hall door. His coffee finished, he then put his mug down, picked up the phone and dialled a number. Then, in a tone of voice we thought we would never ever hear again, responded to the answer at the other end.

'Hello Jonathan. It's Peter here. How are you?'

As Peter listened to Jonathan, John and I daren't move, fearing that Peter might hear us and, aware that he was in full view of us, stop what he was doing.

'I'm doing OK thanks' he then said. 'Actually Jonathan, I have been wondering about the job you offered me. I'd like to take you up on it.'

He listened for a moment or two, then said 'That would be great. I'll be there on Monday morning. See you then. Thanks Jonathan.'

He then put the receiver down and came into the kitchen and put his mug on the drainer.

'Well done, Peter' John said, smiling all over his face. 'It could be just what you need.'

'Well we'll just have to see, won't we?' Peter said.

'I'd better go and get my hair cut I suppose.'

He went back up to his room then reappeared with his jacket. 'I'm off for a walk' he said. Then he was gone. For the first time in a very long time I resisted the temptation to follow him. I made a fresh pot of tea and John and I beamed at one another, each thinking that perhaps at long last the tide was on the turn.

CHAPTER 10

November Continued – December 1995

Peter began work the following Monday, and although it was difficult for him to get up early in the mornings, it said much for his inner strength that he managed to do so.

We wondered how he would cope with working with the general public again after living almost as a recluse, but to our amazement we were to learn from Jonathan during the first week, that Peter was working very hard and coping admirably.

Over the following days I found that time to myself was heavenly. I wallowed in the freedom of having a kind of normality in my life again, even though it was for just a few hours a day. I phoned Mike and our mothers to let them know that Peter was working, and enjoyed a long overdue lunch out with friends. I treated myself to a couple of new outfits and, with Christmas on the horizon, bought a few cards. I slept better than I had in months and my appetite improved.

Peter had been arriving home in the evenings very tired, as we expected. There still, in its various familiar forms, was his depression. He chose not to talk about the job, nor did we press him. We could wait. He would tell us in time. We had learned to live with the way that he was and to be there for him. We expected nothing in return. Once again, after only five days, we were to be tried and tested. For there was to be another shock.

Peter was normally home at around six o'clock each evening. He would eat and then would spend the remainder of the evening in his room or watching TV. But on the Friday evening of that week it was well after nine when we heard his car pull up in the drive. We thought perhaps Jonathan had asked him to work over, for he had told John they were very busy. We had nursed a vague hope that having managed to get through working for five days Peter would be so pleased he had managed to cope, that we might even get a hint of a smile out of him that evening. We knew only too well not to expect more but in those days, even a hint of a smile mattered to us. But Peter came in through the door and, struggling to keep his balance, he leaned with his back to the sink, casually threw his car keys on the draining board and stood looking at us, a sickly grin on his face. He was hopelessly drunk.

It could be argued that after his months of suffering he might want to drown his sorrows in drink from time to time. I had read an article about depressives and alcohol. Many of them drink occasionally because when all else is failing, this lifts them out of their misery and into what they feel and appreciate is a normality. But Peter was far beyond that.

Sarah had said that she had had problems with Peter and his drinking but it had never been an issue since he had been with us because he had had no money of his own. We had given him money for haircuts and his basic essentials and as far as we knew it worked well, but we had never, ever seen him like this.

I thought of the article as I sat there feeling angry yet sorry for Peter, hoping that what we were witnessing was just a 'one off', a circumstance to be forgiven and soon forgotten, but we would have to wait and see.

Peter waited for one of us to speak. I bit my tongue. John said 'Been celebrating, Peter?' He pointed at our wine glasses, his hand wavering. 'Looks like you have. G'night' he said in a slurred voice. With that he staggered across the kitchen and through to the hall, knocking into the hall table as he made for the stairs up to his room, then slamming the door.

Stunned, neither of us could speak; our hopes dashed as realisation dawned.

The only reason Peter had decided to work was to earn money so that he could drink. He had manipulated us. It was as simple as that.

The night Peter came home drunk was the first of many. Incredibly, although he suffered with hangovers, he would manage to get up the next morning and drive to work. Fearful of his drink-driving, we learned that he would drive from Skipton to our village when he finished work, then park at our village pub where he would then begin his binge drinking. The pub was just a couple of hundred yards from our home and he would walk home from there. He at least had the presence of mind to realise the foolishness in drink-driving.

We pleaded with him to think about what he was doing and explained to him that drinking would make him worse. But it was all to no avail.

He looked pale and ill and was deteriorating even further in front of our eyes, but nothing we said or did would stop him from going his own way.

'I'm working. What more do you want?' he would say. 'I'm not your little boy. Leave me alone.'

One day, angry with Peter for all he was putting us through, John said 'If you are not our little boy and are so unhappy here, why don't you move out?'

I thought at the time that it was cruel to challenge Peter in such a way when he was so ill, but John's words had the desired effect. Peter's wordless response spoke realms. At times he would look at us with such overwhelming hatred and could be so morose it was frightening. But always we saw his torment. We would often lie at night unable to sleep, talking over his young life. Perhaps we had got it wrong somewhere in his childhood. Yet his brother was fine.

He had given up talking to us as he had in the days he was first with us. He would never say a word about his days at work although Jonathan insisted, when John phoned and enquired, that Peter was still coping. As always, he stroked his chin, back and forth, back and forth, as his misery became more and more acute through those miserable days and weeks.

Peter's terrible drinking bouts continued and although he still managed to work, we could never comprehend how. He seemed to be locked in a world of his own from which he and we began to feel that we would never escape. Watching him suffer became so painful that, incredible as it may seem, John and I began to think that Peter would not be at peace with himself ever again and that the only way he would find it would be to finally take his life. He was as ill as that.

Those terrible weeks finally took their toll on me. For a long time I had been unable to eat properly. Weight was falling off me. My nights were dark, endless and sleepless and I would be tearful over the slightest thing as I yearned for the life Peter and we once had known. I saw our freedom as utterly beyond reach.

One Saturday morning, John had gone across to see his mother. I was in the middle of ironing and suddenly felt as though my life was draining from me. I unplugged the iron and went to our bedroom where, too weary to undress, I climbed into bed and curled up under the duvet. I thought that if I somehow managed to sleep I would feel better, but I lay there staring at the ceiling, listening to the village clock chiming away the hours, sleep evading me. I was contemplating dragging myself out of bed when I felt movement near me. I pulled back the duvet and was amazed to see Peter sitting on the bed looking down at me.

'What's the matter, Mum?' he said solemnly. I momentarily thought I was dreaming.

'I'm tired Peter' I said. 'Just very, very tired.'

'You've still got your clothes on.'

'Yes, I know.'

Peter continued sitting there and rested his hand on my shoulder. Companiably, we listened to the rain beating on the window.

'I'm horrible to you sometimes, aren't I Mum?'

'Yes you are. It's hard. I don't think I can take much more.'

Then the tears came. It was the first time in all those months that Peter had seen me cry. He handed me a tissue from my bedside table. I let go and sobbed as he sat there with me.

My tears over, he then said 'I hate this life. I'm sorry Mum.' With that, he got up and left the room and went into his own, carefully and quietly closing the door behind him. And I slept.

After that, I knew not to expect miracles. Peter continued to be hostile with me, but afterwards, within hours, he would always, without fail, come to me and say 'Sorry Mum.' I clung to those 'sorrys.'

On another occasion, when I could no longer bear to be in the house having to look at Peter's sad face, I grabbed my car keys and drove and drove, eventually pulling into a lay-by to off-load my tears. When I arrived home, John told me that all the time I was out Peter had paced up and down the hall, not going back into his room until he heard my car pull into the drive.

That dreadful routine in our lives continued as did Peter's drinking. It had been three weeks since Peter had seen Dr Lawson and even though Peter was working, it was patently obvious to us that he was no better. John and I had already begun to consider getting a third opinion when Peter came in one evening, as usual the worse for wear, but surprisingly less so than usual. 'I have something to tell you' he said.

'I know I've been rotten to you both. But, I don't seem to be able to stop myself.' Then to our astonishment he put his hands up on each side of his head and said 'I feel as though there is something in my head that makes me behave like I do. Whatever it is, it is stopping me from getting better.'

We were stunned – speechless. He stood looking at us both, needing a response.

'How would you feel about seeing another specialist?' John asked.

'I'll think about it. But now I've told you, I'm going to bed. Goodnight.' He went up to his room and slammed the door.

Our decision had been made for us. We would go for a third opinion. I contacted Dr Briar, who recommended a specialist in Harrogate. 'He is very good and taught me all I know about mental illness' he said. 'His name is Dr Patra. But you will have to pay. He runs a private clinic.'

Having been reassured that we would be more than willing to pay, Dr Briar then wrote us a referral letter. I phoned and managed to arrange an urgent appointment for Peter for the following week. We felt that this would be our last hope. If it failed, thinking about how Peter and we would continue to cope was completely beyond us. By that time, we were in extremis and absolutely convinced that if Peter deteriorated further, he would take his life.

On the Sunday evening of that week, we insisted that Peter come with us to the village Christmas Carol Service. We knew that he would initially refuse, but John challenged Peter with the suggestion that it was the very least he could do for us. Also, John and I were both very keen to go together and didn't want to leave Peter in the house on his own. He very grudgingly agreed to come. The Church was lit with literally hundreds of candles, and there was an enormous tree just inside the entrance. Boxes of gifts and packets and tins of food were piled up at the back of the church, later to be delivered to the homeless hostel in town. The choir in their blue gowns standing in their pews all added to the magic of the scene.

The three of us sat in a small pew at the back of the church.

As the church filled, villagers greeted one another warmly and the three of us, too. Peter, by way of acknowledgement, face solemn, barely nodded in response.

In other circumstances he would have been considered to be rude. But word gets around a village and people knew and understood.

The service was beautiful as always, but there were times when I just couldn't sing for the huge lump in my throat, my emotions running far too high. Peter sat, jaw set, staring straight ahead and not opening his mouth throughout the service.

But how right Peter had been in telling us he felt he had no real control over the way he behaved, for we were to experience more of his punishing behaviour within a couple of days of my making the appointment.

Just three days before he was due to see the specialist, he came home yet again hopelessly drunk, much worse than we had ever seen him. He stood just inside the kitchen door trying to keep his balance, waiting for us to say something. Daring us.

Despite all he had said to us about not being able to help himself he looked so dreadful I broke down in tears.

It was all too much for John.

'Look, Peter' he said. 'Look what you are doing to your mother.'

Peter shrugged his shoulders and sneered at us horribly again, then said

'I don't give a fuck.'

Whether he could help what he had said or not was all forgotten in John's mind as he walked across to Peter, raised his right hand and gave Peter a swipe across his face that sent him reeling.

I couldn't believe my eyes as Peter regained his balance then stood looking at his father, his hand on the side of his face, his eyes wide open in astonishment.

John stood for several seconds and then did what he had needed to do for a very long time. He cried. And he cried.

He was both mortified and heartbroken.

Peter stood and looked at his father for an age, before

staggering out of the room, without another word. That night I lay awake listening to John as he slept soundly. He had worked through much of the time that Peter had been with us. I had envied him those days and his escape from it all. But that night I had seen and understood for the first time how hard he must have had to work at being strong for me, despite all that he, too, had been going through. He was completely exhausted and had had enough.

The following day Peter looked far worse than he had ever looked in the mornings after his binges. He amazed me by saying just before he left for work

'Dad hit me last night, didn't he?'

'Yes Peter, he did.' I said. I waited for more but without another word he was gone out of sight before John appeared. That next morning John had to leave very early as he had to drive to Birmingham where he was then staying overnight. He looked pale and I had to encourage him to eat breakfast before he left. Not surprisingly he had no appetite.

'Will you be all right?' he said as he prepared to leave.

'Yes,' I lied. 'Don't worry about me.'

That evening Peter came in through the kitchen door much earlier than usual. He took his rucksack to his room then came back into the kitchen and said
'I'm going to see Dr Briar.'

'Why?' I said. But my question hung in the air unanswered as he walked out of the door. Some ten minutes later I was preparing dinner and hoping that Peter might join me when the phone rang. I wiped my hands and picked up the phone in the hall.

'Hello Mrs. Hindle, it's Dr Briar here.' He said 'I'm sorry but

Coming to Terms

I'm afraid you will have to get Peter to the hospital as soon as you can. He has just told me he has taken 25 Paracetamol tablets.'

Stunned and yet somehow not totally surprised, thoughts of John hitting Peter flashed through my mind as I phoned our neighbour. I knew I would be in no fit state to drive. I explained what had happened and asked him if he could run Peter and me to the hospital. He was more than willing. We drove to the surgery which fortunately is only a very short distance from where we live. Peter insisted I sit in the back of the car with him, and, as though acknowledging my weariness, he reached for my hand and held it all the way the hospital.

Once again he was admitted to the medical ward.

Again the doctor told me that they would monitor Peter carefully, but it was thought that he was in no real danger. Peter had told him that he had taken the Paracetamol tablets over a period of a few hours and therefore many of them would already have been absorbed and passed through his system.

I phoned John later that evening and told him all that had happened. He was still upset because he had hit Peter, but together we concluded that although Peter had overdosed and despite him telling us he felt he had no control over his actions we agreed that on this occasion he must have known precisely what he was doing. Once again he had managed to get right away from us, perhaps for our own sakes as well as his own.

I phoned the hospital the next morning and was told that I could collect Peter and bring him home. Before I left to do so, I phoned the clinic and spoke to Dr Patra's secretary to let her know that Peter had been hospitalised. Peter's appointment was for 3 days time, but although he was coming home again his behaviour had become so irrational I was beginning to feel afraid of what he might do to himself. She phoned me back within five minutes.

'Hello Mrs. Hindle' she said. 'It's Janet here again, Dr Patra's secretary. I have spoken to him about Peter and he says that he can't see him during the day today as he has a full diary of patients to see. But he will come in this evening and will phone you once he is here. You can then bring Peter over to see him. Dr Patra feels it is essential he sees Peter as soon as possible.'

A voice from Heaven. I thanked Janet profusely, and then drove over to collect Peter from the hospital. I went up to the ward and to his bed, but he was missing. No one knew where he was. A nurse went looking for him and asked me to sit and wait by his bed. He had packed his bag and it was on the foot of his bed. I tried not to feel concerned but it was almost fifteen minutes before he appeared. I knew he had been deliberately playing games with me, manipulating again, and there was an almost triumphant look in his eyes as he glanced at me and picked up his bag. He spoke not a word as I drove him home.
Nor did he speak to me for the rest of the day. John arrived home from Birmingham early in the evening. We couldn't eat. Peter refused food and went to his room, only to re-appear again very soon. He went through to the back of the house and sat on the doorstep looking out onto the cold night. I suggested he put on a warm coat but he just shot me a look, but after an hour he came back into the house shivering.

The wait for the telephone call from the clinic that night seemed interminable as later the three of us sat in the lounge quite unable to concentrate on anything, each lost in thought as the clock on the mantelpiece ticked away one long hour after another. Just before ten o'clock, the phone rang.

John picked up the phone. 'Hello' he said anxiously.

'Yes it is.'

'No problem' he then said. 'It's very kind of you to see Peter at this hour. I understand you have had a long day. We will be there in twenty minutes, Dr Patra, and thank you'.

CHAPTER 11

December 1995

Was it really Christmas?

The decorated tree was the first thing we saw as the three of us walked into the waiting room of the clinic that night. This was a very different setting to the waiting rooms we had known over the previous three years. This was private medicine. Yet I felt no small amount of guilt as we settled down in comfortable chairs to await the specialist, in this tastefully decorated, thickly carpeted room. The furniture was elegant and there were oil paintings on the walls, and, along the back wall, a table, on which there was a jug of fresh, hot coffee. In the centre of the room there was another table on which was a selection of glossy magazines and a visitors' book. No rows and rows of uncomfortable plastic chairs. Or notice boards and umpteen leaflets giving information on facilities available in the Health Service. No torn, thumbed, years out-of-date magazines and polystyrene cups of coffee or tea sitting on formica topped tables, stained with rings of spilt liquid. No rubbish bins spilling over, staff too busy even to notice, as they struggled through the seemingly endless queues. What possible glimmer of hope could their patients feel in such circumstances?

I felt guilt about the countless souls who in their desperate attempts at seeking reprise from their wretchedness and misery would probably never have the hope and opportunity we felt we might have as we waited in that room that night. Because we could pay. But here we were, and guilt or not, this was surely our last possible hope for Peter.

He sat down as far away from us as possible and appeared not in the least interested in these new circumstances, his mind miles away. I can remember smiling at him, but he simply looked through me. I was used to it, although it hurt no less.

Only moments after we had settled ourselves, the specialist appeared and introduced himself, apologising for keeping us waiting, but we were so thankful to see him we would have waited all night.

Dr Patra had a gentle voice and manner about him. He was of medium height, fairly stockily built, his blue black hair tinged with grey, and had a most pleasant face. His dark rimmed glasses somehow emphasized his kindly eyes.

He invited Peter into his consulting room and suggested we might like to pour ourselves a coffee whilst we were waiting. Head down, shoulders drooping, Peter followed him and closed the door.

John and I sat in companionable silence, knowing our thoughts were in complete unison. After a while I poured coffee we didn't really want, and we both flicked through magazines mechanically and unseeingly. We could hear the muffled sounds behind that heavy door, of the doctor talking gently to Peter. After what seemed an interminable silence, during which I could feel my heart beating, Peter began talking. Slowly and hesitantly at first, then as though gathering momentum, he talked on, and on. I would have given the earth to hear all that he was saying.
I can remember feeling an overwhelming desire to walk into that room and tell the doctor all he had been through.

I was afraid Peter might miss something out. I wanted to tell the doctor about the desolation, the pain, the despair, the anger, the heartache, the misery, the fear and hopelessness. I wanted the man to hear of every single moment of torment Peter had been through over the previous three years, if there was to be a glimmer of a chance that he could be cured of the terrible malignant suffering that had eaten away at so much of his precious young life.

But we had to simply sit and wait.

After some time, we could vaguely make out that the doctor was asking Peter questions, which he answered briefly. We then made out the sound of paper being shuffled and assumed it was the doctor reading through the referral letter and the long lists of medication Peter had been prescribed since his first breakdown.

The quiet seemed to be endless. My anxiety becoming almost unbearable, I glanced at the open visitors' book, and became absorbed in reading through the many comments and signatures and addresses. People had travelled great distances to see this man. His secretary had told me the day before that he had helped literally hundreds to lead normal lives again. There it was, in black and white, a multitude of expressions of gratitude.

Eventually and at last, the door opened and Peter came out and without looking at us, sat down. I searched for a look of relief on his face. There was nothing. Dr Patra then came to the door and invited John and I into his consulting room and asked us to sit down. I held my breath, afraid to listen to what he had to say.

He said simply, and slowly 'Your son is very depressed. I will need to admit him. I can get him better.'

His conviction was absolute. There was no doubt at all in his mind that that was exactly what he could do. He could get Peter better. Just three short sentences. But to John and I they were the most positive words we had heard in three years. We looked at one another, words unnecessary, and our relief immense, speechless.

Coming to Terms

Knowing that we needed time to absorb what he had just said, the specialist then glancing at the notes in front of him, picked up his phone and dialled a number. He then said 'Hello Mark, Sassi here.' It was our GP. 'I have Peter Hindle with me. He has Bipolar Disorder Mark. Bipolar Disorder. I am going to admit him in the morning.' He then continued, enlightening our GP as to how he had come to his conclusions, using medical terminology completely foreign to us, and then instructing the doctor as to the phone calls and arrangements he would have to make first thing the following morning. We sat there half listening, collecting our thoughts. Bipolar Disorder. Little did we know that once we had learned its implications, all our lives would change radically, from then on.

Coming to the end of this conversation, the specialist and our GP exchanged a few brief pleasantries before Dr Patra put down the telephone. He looked again at the letters and lists in front of him, and then told us that there was no way that Peter would have ever responded to any of the medication he had been given. He then surprised us by expressing the view that Peter should have been diagnosed long ago. Referring to the psychiatrist Peter had seen the month previously, and slapping with the back of his hand the papers in front of him, he said,

'Dr Lawson should have diagnosed this. She should have seen. She was my registrar. I taught her. I will have a word with her.' I can recall thinking and wondering at that point why the psychiatrist in Brighton had missed the diagnosis too.

I remembered his words so clearly.

I will never, ever forget them.

'I have told Peter he must pull himself together and get a job. Or he will be unemployable for the rest of his life.'

There was so much we wanted to know and say, and our gratitude was so enormous. John and I began by thanking the doctor profusely. He simply smiled and nodded wisely. He knew. But before we could say more, he stood up and began gathering together the notes in front of him, whilst explaining the arrangements for Peter's admission the next day, and we realised we would have to wait. There would be another time. Also the hour was late and Dr Patra had a long drive home ahead of him and had come a long way to see Peter. I could look up Bipolar Disorder at the library, before we saw him again.

Dr Patra then led us to the door, and back into the waiting room where he gathered up his overcoat and walked with us to the main clinic door. He then turned to look at Peter, who was following behind, head down, hands in pockets. He smiled kindly at him and said

'Young man, you look like an out-of-work undertaker.
When I have finished with you, you will be playing football and chasing the girls again.'

And he has been a man of his word.

CHAPTER 12

December Continued 1995

None of us spoke a word in the car on the 20 minute drive home.

We all knew that there would be much more to face, especially for Peter. Surely nothing could be as testing for us ever again as the three awful years he and we had been through.

On arriving home Peter walked into the house and without a word went straight to his room and, as though ending a chapter in his life, firmly closed the door.

For the first time in as long as we could remember, John and I slept soundly, right through the night.

The following morning we were up early and as instructed John phoned the clinic. He was told that we would be contacted as soon as a bed was available, probably later that morning. He then phoned Jonathan to let him know that Peter wouldn't be at work for the foreseeable future and why. Jonathan told John that he was sorry as he would miss Peter and expressed his surprise, as although he had noticed that Peter had been particularly quiet recently, he could find no fault in the way he had worked.
From all we had been able to glean from Jonathan over the weeks that Peter had been working for him, his demeanor had been fine. Considering the contrasting way he had behaved at home, evidently Peter had been a Jekyll and Hyde.

John then said that he would cancel a meeting in order to take Peter to the clinic, but I knew that the meeting was especially important to him and I insisted that he should go. Perhaps that day would mark the easing of those pressures.

Peter refused breakfast and we heard him moving around in his room, then showering. Drawer and wardrobe doors opened and closed, coat hangers clicked as he packed his bag. Again, he would be glad to get away from us, but this time it was to be different. He was going to get better. He could begin to look to the future.

Without as much as a glance at John and I, he came into the kitchen and made himself a coffee, then took it into the lounge. John prepared to leave, and then after I had again reassured him that I would be all right, we went into the lounge.

Peter was sat staring into space.

'I'm just off to work Peter, so lots of luck' John said. 'And I'll come and see you. You are going to be in very good hands.'

'I suppose so' said Peter, looking at his father and shrugging his shoulders.

'I'm so glad that Dr Patra has got to the bottom of this. You've suffered long enough.'

Peter took a sip of his coffee and said nothing.

John looked at me and slowly shook his head saying 'I'll phone you later, love. I hope all goes well today.'

He gave me a peck on the cheek and left.

The morning seemed interminable and the atmosphere tense as we waited for the call from the clinic. At one point Peter went out into the garden where he wandered around aimlessly, head down, hands in pockets, kicking the occasional stone, every so often looking up at the house.

Coming to Terms

He could settle to nothing and neither could I.

After what had seemed to be an endless morning the call came. Peter almost ran to his room for his bag. He said not a word as I drove him to the clinic where he was warmly welcomed by the receptionist. After taking a few details she phoned the ward and moments later a male nurse appeared and shook hands with us both as he introduced himself as Malcolm. Peter managed a smile as he introduced me.

The nurse then said 'I've been assigned to look after you Peter. If you would like to follow me, I will show you up to your room and you can unpack. Your mother can come too, if you like.'

At that point I felt it would be diplomatic to leave.

Peter shot me a look. I knew only too well that I wouldn't be wanted and as I declined the offer, noted the look of relief on his face.

'I'll leave you to it Peter' I said. Then, thanking Malcolm, made my way to the door. As I did so I looked back. Peter was following Malcolm up the wide staircase without so much as a backward glance.

CHAPTER 13

December Continued 1995

The relief of knowing Peter was with professionals who would observe and care for him was enormous.

As I drove home the sun came out for the first time in days, as though acknowledging a new optimism.

On arriving home, I made myself a drink and sat and wrote a letter to Dr Briar thanking him for referring Peter to Dr Patra. I then phoned Mike and our two mothers, to let them know that we had, at last, got a diagnosis. I broke down and wept tears of joy as I told my closest friend Dorothy.

'Someone has listened at last' I said.

She had been a tremendous source of comfort at times when I had off-loaded to her my heartaches, for I had withheld much from the family.

I then went to Peter's room and sat on his bed for some considerable time, collecting my thoughts. I was mentally and physically drained. I then slowly and methodically stripped his bed, tidied his room and gathered up his washing, wondering as I did so, whether his behaviour towards me would be any different when he came home from the clinic.

I had no appetite for lunch and little energy for doing anything more. I sat by the fire with a book I had been trying to concentrate on for weeks. I gave up and drifted off to sleep, but was awakened by John who had arrived home much earlier than usual.

He too was very tired. I made a cup of tea and we both sat and dozed by the fire for the rest of the afternoon. We made dinner together and opened a bottle of wine by way of celebration. It was good to be on our own again, but we said little as we ate dinner. It was as though we had forgotten how to relax; we were so used to the tension of watching the door for Peter's arrival home and the stress that would ensue.

Christmas was just four days away. My mother and Mike and Zoe must have been collaborating on our behalf, for they had phoned us a couple of weeks previously and told us that no matter how things were, they were coming to us for Christmas to help us through. At that time we couldn't comprehend how we would cope, but with this new set of circumstances I felt that a different focus would be good for John, and I and began to look forward to seeing them all.

There was much to do, but Peter was still foremost on my mind as I drove into town to very belatedly start some Christmas shopping. I had decided to call in at the clinic en-route to see Peter and check that he had all that he needed. The receptionist directed me up the staircase which led firstly to the nurses' station on the right of an enormous open lounge. There were three huge leather settees arranged round a coffee table on which were piles of magazines and daily newspapers. On the shelf below were a variety of games, Monopoly and Scrabble and an assortment of paperback books. On a table by a window was a half-finished jigsaw puzzle. The walls were lined with bright and calming pictures. Malcolm, the nurse I had met the previous day, greeted me and directed me to Peter's room which was the first of several that led off from a long corridor.

Peter opened the door to my gentle knock and with an expressionless face said

'Come in. I thought you would come.'

I sat down in a chair by the window facing his bed. He lay

down on his bed with his hands behind his head, just staring at the ceiling. I felt like an intruder.

'I've come to see if there's anything you need, Peter'.

'No thanks' he said curtly.

'Are you settling in all right?'

He nodded.

'They're all very nice. They've taken some blood and I'm going for a chest X-Ray, then I'm having a brain scan.' Then still staring at the ceiling he said solemnly 'See if I've got a brain I suppose.'

I wasn't sure whether he was trying to cheer me or not, but I chose to smile anyway.

'Sounds as though they're being very thorough.'

'I suppose so.'

I noticed a book on his bedside table and went over and picked it up. 'What are you reading, Peter?'

He snatched it from me.

'I don't think you should read that' he said.

'One of the patients has loaned it to me. She's got the same complaint as me. Bipolar Disorder. That's the medical term for manic depression,' and then, as though disgusted with himself, he said 'That's what I've got.'

'Yes, I know Peter. It's hard for you and I'm sorry. But Dr Patra says he can get you better.'

'Well we'll just have to see, won't we?' he said in such a

bitter tone I felt more and more uncomfortable.

'Have you remembered that your brother is coming up for Christmas?'

'Yep' was all I got in reply. I got up to leave. He didn't move.

 'Dad sends his love. I'll see you tomorrow.'

I waited, still he didn't move.

I walked out and quietly closed the door.

The book was entitled 'Coping with Elation and Depression.' It was the first thing I bought in town that day, and the first of many books and articles I was to read over the following months as I learned as much as I could about manic depression.

Thanks to Mike, Zoe and my mother and their company we had an enjoyable Christmas. They all worked hard in their various ways to make sure of it, and were particularly good with Peter, who was allowed out for the day, recognising that for the most part he was best left alone, just to observe all that was going on.

Jacob was the focus of much attention, fascinated with all that was happening around him on his first Christmas. It was noticeable that in contrast to our holiday in Scotland when Peter was contented to have Jacob sitting on his knee, his mental state had deteriorated to such an extent that he was only vaguely interested in his nephew's lively activities, or any of ours.

Mike and Zoe drove Peter back to the clinic on Boxing Day. He was glad to go, and Mike told us that at the clinic Peter greeted Malcolm as though he was an old friend and his whole demeanor changed. He was amongst people who could help and understand him, where we had tried so hard and failed.

CHAPTER 14

January 1996

Christmas over, in the days that followed, John and I would take turns visiting Peter. Often when we arrived he would be sitting on one of the settees reading, or talking to other patients. They were encouraged to get together and socialise rather than linger alone in their rooms, and there was always a nurse on duty at the station observing or available for conversation. The place had a quiet, relaxed atmosphere.

By that time, Peter had had a series of medical tests including a chest X-Ray and brain scan. He had also commenced taking Lithium. I had already read and learned by then it was the suggested and historically successful treatment for Bipolar Disorder. He had been prescribed Seroxat which is also given for depression. Dr Patra felt that a combination of the two would keep Peter sufficiently balanced. Additionally Peter was having one-to-one counselling daily and regular group therapy as part of the on-going treatment. Dr Patra visited him daily.

John and I had every confidence in the carers and believed that Peter, with patience and determination, would come through.

In the meantime, John and I were making the best of our relatively new freedom. One bright, crisp sunny morning, two weeks into January, we were preparing for a long overdue walk in the Dales when the phone rang and to my surprise it was Peter.

'It's me' he said in his usual flat tone of voice. 'What are you and Dad doing tomorrow?'

It was the first time he had phoned us in months.

'We are going to have our usual roast lunch, Peter, and then if it's a nice afternoon we'll be going for a walk. Why do you ask?'

'Dr Patra says I can come out for the day and I'd like to bring a friend. She's a patient here as well.'

My mind went back momentarily to the call he had made to us just after he had met Sarah. How different this was.

'Well, would you like to bring your friend for lunch?'

'Yes please. If it's all right.'

'Of course it is, Peter. It's an excellent idea. Do you want picking up?'

'No thanks. She's got a car. Oh, and by the way, she's got the same complaint as me.'

'I see' I said, trying not to sound concerned, unsure whether this would be the right kind of friendship to encourage.

'I'll make the meal for about 1 o'clock. Roast beef and Yorkshire pudding. One of your favourites.'

'Fine. She's called Jane' he said abruptly and rang off.

We enjoyed a walk that day in glorious weather. Perhaps Peter's call had enhanced it, although we had doubts about his new-found friend. We drove to Hebden, and parked the car, then followed the track that leads high up and over the hills. The views there are wonderful. Dotted here and there are grazing sheep, and streams leading down to the valley and the river. In Grassington we ate our packed lunch before making our way back along the river to the car. It had always been one of our favourite walks, and to get right away was just what we both needed. The feeling of freedom was Heaven.

The following day, Peter and Jane arrived minutes before 1 o'clock. Peter introduced her and she gave us the sunniest of smiles.

Jane is tall, slim and pretty and has a head of short, neat wavy auburn hair. She looked neat and tidy and was dressed in a simple, plain, pale blue sweater and black trousers that flattered her long legs. I noticed that her nails were painted bright red.

'Pleased to meet you. It's kind of you to let me come for lunch' she said. Her eyes looked so bright; it was hard to imagine that she was ill too.

'You're very welcome' I said. John glanced across at me wide-eyed, equally surprised by her.

He then suggested that she might like to go out and look at our garden and see the view, whilst I put the finishing touches to lunch. She followed him outside.

Peter stayed inside and stood with his hands in his pockets, leaning on the kitchen door frame.

'She's nice, isn't she?' he said with barest of smiles.

'If first impressions are anything to go by, yes she is, Peter.'

'She's the one that loaned me that book. I like talking to her.'

'Good' I said 'Are you finding it helpful?' hoping he would say more.

'Yes' was all I got in reply.

But that was it, and I had learned from bitter experience not to expect much from him, then I wouldn't be disappointed. As I spooned and drained vegetables into tureens, I could feel his eyes on me and felt discomfited. I longed to know what was going on in his mind.

I was relieved to be able to ask him to let John and Jane know that lunch was ready. Jaw set, Peter walked out to the garden.

Lunch wasn't as difficult as I feared it might be. Jane seemed confident and talkative and told us that she had been diagnosed and admitted to the clinic just a week before Peter. She had worked for the Halifax Building Society until she became too ill to cope. Her parents lived in Liverpool and she had a house in Halifax. She had been through a very difficult time but didn't elaborate on that. Finally she said

'I was desperate when I was admitted to the clinic. I feel safe there.'

I wondered whether Peter felt the same and looked across at him, but he was concentrating on eating his meal. His face gave nothing away, but it was good to see him enjoying his food.

As Jane talked, John and I warmed to her and any doubts that we might have had about her being the wrong kind of friend for Peter disappeared in that short time. The meal over, Peter said sharply 'I think we should be going.'

Jane looked across at him. 'But we've only just finished Peter. I'd like to help your mother clear up before we go ' she said firmly.

Her tone of voice was almost challenging. Peter, resigned, shrugged his shoulders and went up to his room. John, suggesting he leave us to it, picked up the Sunday papers and went through to the lounge.

Jane was easy company and talked away as we worked together in the kitchen loading the dishwasher and washing the saucepans. During the course of our conversation, I noted that she touched briefly on the fact that Peter had told her all about Sarah and that he was no longer fretting for her. Jane told me that she was married but separated from her husband and that the marriage was definitely over. She knew much about John's and my working backgrounds and also about Mike, Zoe and Jacob in Cornwall. It became clear that she and Peter had spent a lot of time in each other's company at the clinic. As she talked, I warmed to her more and more, feeling grateful that Peter had perhaps found a friend who he could talk to and value. Hopefully, she might begin to value him, too.

John reappeared and suggested she might like to see a painting we had of our view we had commissioned an artist to paint for us a few years previously. 'I'd love to' she said keenly, then followed John through to the hall.

Peter must have been listening in his room for the kitchen noises to stop, for as I was wiping over the oven top he appeared at the kitchen door and again stood watching me. I concentrated very hard on what I was doing, biting my tongue again. As I finished and was drying my hands he said

'Thank you Mum. Can I bring Jane again?'

'Of course you can' I said, delighted that he had actually said something nice.

'She'd be very welcome.'

He then called through to Jane in the hall.

'I'd like to go now, Jane.' Then, in an almost pleading

manner, and louder 'Please.'

'All right, Peter' she said, not in the least fazed by the way he had spoken to her. She picked up her bag and collected her car keys from the hall table and made for the door, and as she did so said,

'Thank you for lunch. I've appreciated coming today. I hope I can come again.'

I told her that she would be very welcome and meant it very sincerely. John and I then walked them out to the car. Only Jane waved as they drove away.

Little did we know that from that day she was to play a very significant part in our lives.

After that first Sunday, Peter started to bring Jane over to see us every few days and we looked forward to seeing her. She told us that she was also taking Lithium, felt better for the treatment and counselling at the clinic and her specialist had said that she could begin to think of going home. Her mother, Eileen, who lived in Liverpool, visited her every few days and would stay with Jane at the clinic. Jane brought her over to meet me one afternoon when she came over with Peter. He and Jane went off for a walk and Jane's mother and I were glad of the opportunity to confide in one another and empathise.

We were both coming to terms with the cruel complaint. But Eileen was grieving too, over the break-up of Jane's marriage, more so it seemed than Jane herself. Jane was their only child and the stress and sadness of it all were even harder for her to bear.

After three weeks in the clinic and whilst Jane was very positive, we saw no change in Peter's behaviour or his attitude towards us. He still spoke very little and somehow just tagged along with Jane, glad of her company. We had no problem with that as we thought that perhaps her determination to get through would eventually become an example to him. As far as we could tell, he was still seriously depressed and gave us not the slightest impression that he was making any real effort.

Providing they attended all the therapy and counselling classes, Peter and Jane were allowed out of the clinic whenever they wished. We noticed that they were spending all their free time together, often calling across to see John and I, although we were convinced that the visits were of Jane's instigation, for Peter rarely spoke to us on those visits.

After a four week stay in the clinic, Jane was discharged and went back home to Halifax. I would telephone her every few days and occasionally call over to see her. She still kept in regular touch with Peter. She had decided that she would begin by decorating her front lounge. Her determination was incredible.

'I must have a purpose' she would say. 'Something positive to do.'

Peter was discharged and back home with us at the end of the third week in January. We had hoped that he might have been easier to live with but were disappointed, for the only real difference we could see was that he was no longer drinking. He looked pale and drawn and would still shut himself away in his room for hours on end, and although we had known from the beginning that recovery would take time, we were anxious to see signs of change, no matter how small. I noticed in his room a diary. Jane told me that patients on discharge were advised to keep a daily account of their feelings and moods which the psychiatrist could then read and refer to on their 'follow up' appointments.

I was relieved to see that Peter was taking his Lithium as

prescribed. On the one occasion I foolishly ventured to tell him so, his reaction was so vitriolic I regretted it bitterly.

John too was having difficulty, but admitted that in many ways those days were harder for me and suggested that as soon as it could be arranged I must have a break and go down to Cornwall for a few days to see Mike and Zoe and Jacob again. He made a point of telling Peter that that was what I was going to do, in the hope that it might move Peter's thoughts away from himself.

Also, he suggested that he should begin to consider going back to work as he had been advised. They were difficult days and I constantly reminded myself that whilst I was struggling to come to terms with Peter's cruel complaint, so was he.

Jane proved to be the only light in our lives through that time. Peter was still in daily touch with her and would spend hours talking to her on the phone. Every weekend he would drive over to see her, and it was only then that we would feel any relief from the atmosphere that still enveloped our home. But even those episodes of relief were to be short lived.

CHAPTER 15

February 1996

Jane's 30th birthday was on February 1st and, stoical as ever, she had decided that she was going to take the opportunity to catch up with a few friends and go out for a celebratory meal. She invited Peter to go over to Halifax and join them, suggesting that he could stay overnight. It was the first social occasion that Peter had been to for months and we felt that it would be good for him. But our hopes were dashed once more when on the Saturday morning, the day after Jane's birthday, there was a call from Jane.

'I'm phoning to let you know that Peter's in hospital.'

'He's what?' I said incredulously.

'He seemed to be reasonably all right when he left here on Thursday morning. Has he gone down again? Is he back in the clinic, Jane?'

'Oh no. He's in hospital here in Halifax. He didn't go to work yesterday. He kept being violently sick, there was blood in his vomit and he had a blinding headache, so I sent for the doctor, I was so worried about him.'

I struggled to take it all in.

'What do they say is wrong with him Jane?'

'They think it's gastro-enteritis but they're not sure. He's on the men's medical ward in the General.'

'I'm so sorry you've had all this Jane. What about you? Are you all right?'

'I'm OK, I'm just tired, but I was disappointed that Peter had to leave my celebration early. He was getting on quite well with everyone, and then suddenly said he didn't feel well and he left.'

'Well thank you for letting us know about him, Jane. Look, don't worry. We'll be over later this morning.'

I told her to take care, thanked her again, put the phone down and wondered what we would do without her.

I walked wearily back into the kitchen. I told John all that Jane had said and slowly began to clear away my breakfast. There it was again. That lump in the pit of my stomach. Also, I was convinced that the diagnosis of gastro-enteritis was wrong. It just didn't seem to fit with Peter.

I also remember feeling a huge disappointment. Cornwall would now be out of the question.

What's gastro-enteritis?' asked John, positive as ever, wanting to clarify the facts.

'It's inflammation of the stomach lining and intestine. The symptoms are vomiting and headache and it can be caused by stress, or a food allergy of some sort, sometimes food poisoning. Perhaps the doctors are right, but I can't get my head round this diagnosis somehow.'

'Whatever it is, you are going to Cornwall, or you'll be in hospital next. We'll sort something out.'

I protested, but he was adamant. I decided not to argue, at least for the time being.

We set off for Halifax later that morning.

CHAPTER 16

February Continued 1996

The General reminded me of the hospital where I had trained in Norwich in the late fifties. Like many of the old Victorian hospitals it was depressing and cheerless, with its tall, dark, red brick buildings and umpteen redundant chimneys. Inside were endless corridors. Leading off them to the right and left, were the wards, lined on each side with their long rows of beds. Some patients were sitting beside them, others lying in their beds, too ill to sit out, get well cards strung up behind them or on their bedside lockers, or propped up between bowls of fruit and vases of flowers.

We located the men's medical. Peter's bed was relatively near the sister's desk, where as is the custom, the more seriously ill can be easily observed. I asked if I could have a word with a doctor and was told that he would be due on the ward shortly. Not really quite sure how or in what kind of state we expected to see Peter, we were ill-prepared, as we approached his bed.

He was as white as death and lying flat on his back, conscious but staring at the ceiling. He had an intravenous drip in his arm. On his bedside locker were a vomit bowl and a box of tissues. Hung just above his head was a notice on which was written in bold words 'Nil by Mouth.'

John and I found it hard to know what to say. We had become accustomed to Peter's manner towards us, and even in these awful circumstances doubted his response if we expressed sympathy of any kind. We greeted him quietly and each pulled up a chair beside his bed.

'I can't talk much. I've got a terrible headache' he said, not moving his head either way to look at us.

I was overwhelmed with pity for him, knowing that if they were not certain of his diagnosis he would be under strict observation. They would give him nothing for his pain, as it would mask his symptoms.

'Don't worry. We'll just sit here quietly.'

He dozed off for a while, and then opened his eyes and his next words took me by complete surprise.

'You must go down to Cornwall, Mum. It's time you had a break and went down to see Mike. You've been looking forward to it.'

John raised his eyebrows and smiled across at me. I was so taken aback by this sudden consideration for me, I almost burst into tears. It was the first time Peter had spoken kindly to me, sensitively, in months. I told him that I would talk to the doctors and then think about it. He seemed satisfied with that and even managed a vague smile, little knowing that there was no way I would even begin to consider such a trip whilst he was so ill. Peter dozed off again. I sat watching the nurses, all very busy, remembering warmly my own nursing days and envying them.

Minutes later, a houseman appeared on the ward. John stayed with Peter whilst I went over to talk to him.

He told me that Peter was to have an urgent CT scan the following morning and that the consultant would see us to discuss the result in the afternoon.

We stayed a while longer and were preparing to leave when Jane walked onto the ward. She said that she had been regularly visiting Peter and would stay with him for a while. We asked about her party and she said it had been good catching up with friends again and that she was going to try and go back to work, just part-time to begin with. I had my doubts; she looked so very tired. A few minutes later, we bade our farewells and made for home, reassuring Peter that we would be visiting again the following afternoon. He didn't react in any way.

The hours dragged on interminably until the next day when we were back at the hospital and waiting anxiously in a side room for the consultant. Like Dr Patra, he was Pakistani and had that same gentle smile and manner. He shook hands with us and indicated that we should sit down.

He told us he had had doubts about the diagnosis of gastro-enteritis the doctors had given Peter on his admission. When called upon to examine Peter he had noticed a bruise behind his right ear. To confirm his suspicions he had requested a head scan. What this had revealed was a clot of blood between the layers of protective membranes that surround the brain.

'I'm afraid your son has what is called a subdural haematoma. You see, your son has had a fall.'

What we were to hear next left us reeling.

The specialist had gleaned from Peter that on the night he had left the party and gone back to Jane's house, he vaguely remembered falling headlong down the stairs and banging his head on a sharp corner of the radiator at the bottom.

There was more. Peter had also confessed that at the party he had had seven pints of a very strong beer. In other words he had fallen because he had been drunk.

The consultant then smiled kindly at us, waiting patiently for us to absorb all he had just told us.

There was no need to put into words what we now knew.

Peter could have died. The fall could have killed him.

Moments later, such was my anger, I had an overwhelming desire to go to Peter's bedside and simply ask him just what next he was going to put us through.

John sighed heavily. 'Thank you doctor' he said. 'This must be frustrating and time-wasting for you.'

The specialist smiled 'It's my job.'

'In a few days time I will be sending your son for another scan, to establish whether the clot is dispersing. In the meantime we will keep Peter on bed rest and regularly check his blood pressure.'

'What about side effects?' I said.

'I don't really expect any, although of course I can't make any promises at this stage.'

Another silence.

'Do you know that our son is a manic depressive?' I was suddenly feeling guilty and aware that this busy man had no need for patients who took up his valuable time unnecessarily, as Peter had done. Perhaps Peter's complaint might suffice as an apology.

'Oh yes' he said, nodding wisely, and then hesitating momentarily, he got up and walked out of the room.

We went back and sat by Peter's bed. Neither of us said a word. He knew what he had done. I wondered whether he felt any remorse, but doubted it very much. Drink had reared its ugly head yet again. How foolish we had been to imagine that he was ready to address and begin to control his need for alcohol, so soon after his diagnosis. But in a very short space of time, whilst sitting there beside his bed, the heartache began again. And I forgave him. He was right. He was only thirty two and he had no life. But what he had, he had almost lost.

We drove home in silence, the weather matching our mood. The sun had disappeared behind low, dark clouds. Snow was forecast.

John was working away from home over the next three days. I reassured him that I would be able to cope, but almost envied him as I waved him off the next morning, and prepared to drive over to the hospital that afternoon. There had been heavy snowfall and the hour's drive over to Halifax was dismal. The snowploughs had been busy and I drove along black, shiny roads piled high on either side with banks of snow and passed blackened derelict houses and now disused mills so typical of some areas of the Pennines. My mind was in turmoil, confused as to why Peter, John and I were being put through all this. I felt as though we were living in a world far distant from anything I had ever known before. Right then, Cornwall was somewhere in a Heaven that I just couldn't imagine in my mind's eye I would ever see again. Michael, Zoe and Jacob were a million miles away.

I kept my visits to Peter short. He didn't really want me there. If he did he never showed it. Attempts at conversation became a waste of time; even though he was beginning to look fractionally better and would talk to and acknowledge the nurses he would barely speak to me. He asked on one occasion whether I was going to Cornwall.

I told him I would think about it when he was better. But the sensitivity he had displayed towards me a few days previously was no longer there. He was kicking me below the belt again. It was all my fault.

How I dreaded those visits. On one occasion driving home, the traffic was busier than usual and I took what I thought would be a good diversionary short cut, only to find myself miles later in the middle of nowhere on a narrow road that just led into blackness. I became frightened and tears streamed down my face as I struggled to manoeuvre a three-point turn before managing to head back to the lights through gridlocked traffic, glad to be back with people again.

Jane was still visiting through this time and I was in regular touch with her by phone, anxious for her to know that she should always be aware that we were there for her too. But despite the reassurances she always gave me, she knew and admitted that there was more to face and that patience was of the essence.

I was glad to have John back home again, and together we drove to the hospital at the weekend. We walked on to the ward to find Peter sitting on the edge of his bed in a dressing gown, but this time he also had a determined look on his face. There was a wheelchair beside his bed.

'Hello' he said, with a nod.

'Take me to the ward downstairs. You can push me in this wheelchair. The nurses are too busy. So they say you can take me.'

'But why, Peter? You're supposed to be on complete bed-rest' John said.

'You'll see' was all we could get out of him.

Calculating his movements, he slowly lowered himself into the wheelchair and, checking first with the ward sister that he had indeed been given permission, we headed for the lift and to the ward below. It was women's medical. Just inside the door, in a bed near sister's desk, lay Jane. Fast asleep. This was beginning to be almost farcical.

Coming to Terms

We carefully and quietly pulled up chairs each side of the bed, sat down and waited. After a while she opened her eyes and smiled at us. Then, in her usual practical and inimitable way she told us slowly and gently that she had 'nosedived' into another depression over the two previous days, and had overdosed. She had then called and told a close friend who had phoned for an ambulance.

Jane then told us that the doctors had said that she could be discharged the next day. But she wasn't to be alone. Immediately I responded,

'You can come home to us if you like, Jane.'

We owed this young woman more than we would ever be able to repay.

'If you're sure' Jane said. 'I need to see my psychiatrist again at the clinic.'

I then asked to speak to her doctor and verified all that Jane had said. With a promise that I would take care of all her tablets, it was agreed that I could take her home with me, after I had visited Peter the next day.

John was due to go away on another business trip and it troubled him that I was having to cope with all this on my own, but there was nothing to do but just plough on through it and take it a day at a time. We stayed a while longer with Jane, before taking Peter back to his ward. If he felt relief that we were going to look after her, he never expressed it. Emotion, as far as we were concerned, seemed to be beyond him.

I picked up Jane the following day, after she had first visited Peter.

Jane, by that time, knew us quite well and so we were all very comfortable in one another's company. As always, she managed to disguise the way she was really feeling. Our admiration and affection for her was huge.

Discussing her one day, John said it was as though an angel had come into our lives.

She settled in with us and managed to eat a light meal that evening.

I heard Jane moving in the night and got up minutes later to find her sitting at the kitchen table, her hands round a mug of tea. I made one for myself and joined her. She talked and talked and appeared to be relieved to off-load all that was on her mind.

She began by telling me that her husband had no longer been able to cope, as when she was depressed she had lain curled up on their settee, day after day for weeks on end. Prior to that she had been 'in charge' of their life together, booking trips away and having their bags packed almost every weekend as she soared higher and higher up in to a manic state before then hitting the depths of despair and desolation and finally her admission to the clinic, and her diagnosis. Her husband had moved into a flat in town and they were now estranged. He had been unable to cope with Jane's erratic behavior and it had cost them their marriage.

The following morning, I drove her to the clinic where after being seen by her specialist, she was re-admitted. The next day, her mother came over to see her and again stayed overnight at the clinic. Jane, by then, was on one-to-one observation.

Two days later, Peter had a repeat scan and as the consultant had predicted, his haematoma had reduced in size. His general condition began to improve and he was allowed to get up and spend more time out of bed each day. We were told that, all being well, he would be discharged home in a few days' time.

That particular February will always remain in my memory as one of the most awful months of my life. The shock and worry of Peter's fall, after all the previous years, months and weeks of trying to cope with him, his illness and attitude towards me, finally took its toll and I knew I was heading for a breakdown. They say that a mother loves unreservedly and I have never doubted it for a moment. But Peter knew it too, that no matter how much he hurt or lashed out at me as he gave vent to his fears and frustrations, I would always turn the other cheek. I had never stopped loving him but I could take no more. I was still losing weight. Tears would spill down my cheeks uncontrollably over nothing at all and I would sit staring into space for hours on end. But I was determined that somehow I would continue to cope. John was worried about me and again urged me to go down to Cornwall, as did Michael and Zoe, who also reminded me that it had been six months since I had seen our little grandson.

I made an appointment to see our GP, who reassured me that as far as he knew from the update he had had from the hospital, there would be no further serious concerns over Peter's head injury and that he would come through.

Jane too, had begun to improve and was expecting to be discharged in the next few days.

I then made my decision. I would go and see my little family whilst Peter was still in care in hospital. I needed to start and think about rebuilding my life, our future, and my strength, if I was to help him when he was discharged home.

Word soon spreads in a village and the support we had from friends and villagers through those awful days was tremendous and heart-warming. There were kindly notes and cards put through the door. Flowers would be left on the doorstep. A friend in the village who had a smallholding phoned and suggested I take Jane up to see their new-born lambs. A couple of days before I left for Cornwall, I picked Jane up from the clinic and took her there. She loved it, and it was a treat to see her losing herself for a while in the little creatures.

There were phone calls offering help of any kind. But all we could do was express our thanks and see it through.

It was a most incredible coincidence that Roger, the husband of my closest friend, Dorothy, a nurse who I had trained with, also suffered with Bipolar Disorder and had done so for several years. At that time, he was stable and on Lithium, but he too had been through a terrible scenario before his diagnosis. The many sympathetic and encouraging letters we had from them both at that time were invaluable.

It was a bitterly cold mid-February morning as I boarded the train in York for the seven-hour journey down to Cornwall. But I had wrapped up well and, armed with some light reading, I was determined to make the best of the trip and enjoy my escape to our little family there. I was sorry John couldn't be with me but he had work to do, and although Peter was being taken care of, we had agreed that no matter what, one of us must be home to visit him in hospital daily and be 'on call'.

At first I noted people laughing and talking around me on the train. It had been such a long time since John and I had had any real fun.

But self-pity would get me nowhere. I made an effort and began exchanging an occasional word with the ever-changing passengers. I would occasionally doze for a while or read, or take in the scenery. It's a pleasant journey down to the West Country, travelling through dramatic, changing scenery and over the various estuaries much further south. My journey at an end, Michael's beaming smile as I stepped down from the train was just the tonic I needed. He gave me a big hug.

'Good to see you, Mum' he said, picking up my case.

'You should have come sooner.'

We headed for his car.

'Now you're going to forget about Peter for a few days and enjoy your little grandson.'

I knew I wouldn't be able to forget Peter, but I did indeed enjoy Jacob. He was already nine months old and I had missed so much of his early development.

I had a wonderful time with him. I walked him for miles in his pushchair, helped Zoe bath him, played with him with his toys and just wallowed in the joy of his young, innocent and uncomplicated company.

I phoned the hospital every morning and was reassured that Peter was still recovering. I decided not to ask to speak to him, lest his coldness upset me all over again and spoil all that I was enjoying. Mike and Zoe were thoughtful and caring. I slept well and sometimes late, and over the five days I was with them I began to feel so much better, although coupled with those feelings were pangs of guilt, for not visiting them for so long. Something I was determined to remedy as soon as Peter was well again.

But also my trip down to Cornwall was to prove to be a turning point. For the night before I left, I had that very significant dream that ended my denial.

The memory of it has crossed my mind many times since, and will never ever be forgotten. Because of it, I left Cornwall knowing that from then on, I would be able to cope with whatever challenges there would inevitably be to face. For there was no doubt in my mind that there would be more.

CHAPTER 17

More of February 1996

During the journey home I was able to collect my thoughts. Peter had been verbally cruel to me through the greater part of the previous two years. We now had a firm diagnosis. As long as I consistently remembered that it was his complaint that had made him behave so badly towards me, I would manage. When his denial was over too, we would be back where we were, enjoying each other's company as we had done before this awful nightmare had begun.

Just two days after my return home, Peter was discharged home from hospital. My respite was over. Jane too, had been discharged from the clinic.

Peter looked terrible. He was still deathly white and the bruise behind his ear, the size of a tennis-ball, was a hideous colour mix of purple, black and dark yellow. He was wearing a baseball cap, and still getting headaches. The doctor had advised him to wear it for a few days to shield his eyes from bright light.

Within a week of being back with us, Peter said one night at dinner

'I'm going back to work next week.'

We were horrified, he still looked so ill. John looked at Peter, and, shaking his head, said

'But you're in no fit state Peter. You don't look well enough.'

'Well I'm not sitting around here all day,' was Peter's response.

I then tried. 'It's too soon, Peter. Please give yourself a few more days.'

Memories of the few and rare kind words he had said to me whilst he was in hospital flashed through my mind and quickly faded as he glared at me.

'I'm not your little boy. I'm big enough to make up my own mind.'

John, not wanting to make a scene said

'If that's how you feel, Peter, you had better phone Jonathan and let him know.'

Peter had made up his mind. We had to look upon it as a positive step, for he had made a decision.

And so he went back to work.

He looked dreadful for the first few days, and although he would arrive home utterly drained he coped and for once proved us wrong. Within a month he looked very much better and his bruise had disappeared.

During the following weeks, Peter and Jane saw each other so regularly that it became clear they had become an 'item' and, consuming more and more of Peter's time, Jane proved to be a blessing. She spent more and more time with us, and although she told us she still suffered with her demons, her manner belied her inner turmoil. She was well aware of Peter's behaviour and attitude towards us and frequently told him so.

'You should feel ashamed of yourself Peter' we once heard her say.

It was during that time that we were relieved to hear word

from Brighton that there had been an offer on Peter's house. We told him so, and attempted to discuss it with him. But by then, thanks to Jane, he dismissed the news with a shrug, was not in the least bit interested and made it quite clear to us that the house and his life in Brighton with Sarah no longer meant anything at all.

'You can deal with the sale. I'm not interested,' was the only comment he made as he closed that chapter in his life.

CHAPTER 18

March 1996

Despite the difference Jane had made to Peter's life we began to think that he was not responding to the Lithium and began to despair of ever seeing him well again. There had been few signs, although once again Jonathan reassured us that he was doing well and working very hard. The turning point finally came just six weeks after his fall and three months after his diagnosis.

One Saturday morning early in March, our village WI were having their annual jumble sale and I was loading up the car boot with bags and boxes of unwanted items to take to the village hall, when Peter came out to me in the drive.

'Would you like me to help you, Mum?' he said.

My jaw must have dropped, I was so astonished. I thought for a moment that I must have been dreaming.

'It would be lovely, Peter. Some of these boxes are quite heavy.'

Without another word but looking very determined, he loaded them into my car boot and then asked what else he could do.

I had arranged to collect jumble from a neighbour and take it to the hall for her.

'It would be a great help if you picked up Marion's jumble and took it to the hall for me. Apparently, she's got loads in her garage.'

'O.K.' he said. 'I'll get my car keys.' With firm strides he walked back into the house.

Coming to Terms

I was so surprised that I forgot what I was doing and just stood staring at the front door, waiting for him to reappear.

When he did so he gave me a hint of a smile as he opened his car door. Once inside, he slammed the door hard and loudly and drove away.

I was so utterly thrilled I ran back into the house to tell John.

I didn't know where he was so I just shouted.

'John, I think he's getting better.' Then before John could respond from wherever he was, I was out of the house again and in my car, driving at great speed to the village hall. This was just too good to miss.

Peter was most helpful that morning and drove back and forth to various houses collecting jumble, and lifting and moving heavy items in the hall where necessary.

He responded cheerfully to greetings and thanks, and as I watched him out of the corner of my eye, I thought I was in Heaven.

But within the space of a few hours and back at home again his smiles faded and he became withdrawn again.

I was not despondent, for it was a start and from that day, just once in a while, he would be more communicative, although still in short snatches and his manner towards me was still distant. Occasionally he would binge and there was nothing we could do but let him learn the consequences. Jane became the focal point in his life and influenced him greatly. She was furious with him when he drank and would let him know in no uncertain terms. She had never had a problem with alcohol.

Despite all the signs that Peter was beginning to respond

to the Lithium, we learned not to become over-optimistic. Even so, we were ill-prepared for what Peter had to say to us one evening at the end of May.

We had finished our evening meal and I had just poured us coffee.

'I have something to tell you. Jane is pregnant.' There was no smile.

He simply blurted the staggering news to us in those two short sentences.

He said it as though making a formal announcement, then sat looking at us waiting for our response. The shock was like a stab wound and in the silence that followed, John and I each waited for the other to say something appropriate.

This should have been wonderful news, but in these alarming circumstances it was the last thing we wanted to hear.

'When is the baby due, Peter?' I said, hoping I didn't look and sound as concerned as I felt.

'At the end of December.' Still no smile.

'Are you both pleased?' This was John.

'I think so.'

Peter had always loved children, and they him. In different circumstances we would be cracking champagne. He waited again for our reaction. Then, suddenly feeling an overwhelming pity for him, I managed a smile and said the words that he must have been hoping for.

'Congratulations, Peter. That's lovely news'.

Coming to Terms

John followed suit.

'We'd better phone and congratulate Jane.' Then, trying to make light of it,

'I'd better start saving up for a pram.'

Peter finally smiled, relief written all over his face.

When I phoned Jane she said 'We've been worrying about telling you; but we will be all right. We'll manage somehow and I've already taken myself off my Lithium.'

Jane sounded to be so genuinely pleased that we had no other course to take but to congratulate her too. We would simply have to cope.

Hiding our worries from Peter and Jane, aware that Bipolar Disorder was genetic, and seriously concerned about Jane and how she would be as she would no longer be taking Lithium, John and I made an appointment to see Dr Patra.

He too, was taken aback at the news, but we were pleasantly surprised and relieved to learn from him that nature would carry Jane through and that she would have no problems with either highs or lows throughout her pregnancy. It was a medical fact, he told us, and also true from his own experience as a psychiatrist that he had known manic depressive women much more seriously affected by the complaint, who would plan to have several children because the pregnancy months were the only time that they felt any psychological normality in their lives.

We left the clinic that day feeling better. But although Jane did indeed cope through those early days of her pregnancy she was not always well. Peter was very concerned about her and she gave him an ultimatum. As soon as he could prove to her that he was no longer drinking, that he could manage his life responsibly and without depending so heavily upon her, he could then move in with her.

Over the weeks that followed, there were noticeable changes in Peter and it became clear that, hard though it was for him, he was making a real effort.

Also at that time, Dr Patra advised him that he should begin to think about moving out. He suggested that he should consider moving into a shared house, so that he would still have company, for although Peter was indeed much better, he still had a lot to learn. He had lived with us for eight months and we were told that we could do no more for him.

CHAPTER 19

July 1996

We had often wondered how and when Peter would have recovered sufficiently to make the decision to move out. Much as John and I had longed for our freedom over the months he was with us, we would never, ever have asked him to leave. Once the decision was taken from him, he appeared to have no problem at all seeking somewhere else to live. He found accommodation within three days and told us that he would be moving out on the Friday morning of that week.

John was away in London at that time and we were sorry that he wouldn't be at home for Peter's last evening with us. However, I looked forward to having dinner with Peter, anticipating that he would be in reasonably good spirits. But I was bitterly disappointed. He was fidgety and stressed and responded to my pleasantries with short, curt replies, and so, for the most part, we ate in silence.

The meal was over. 'Thanks,' he said. 'I'll go and pack.' He went to his room and didn't appear again for the rest of the evening. Moving out wasn't going to be easy for him after all.

July the fifth was a warm and sunny morning. The date will be forever engraved in my mind.

Peter was up much earlier than usual and took his belongings to his car before coming into the kitchen for his breakfast.

I had decided not to speak until I was spoken to.

'Morning' he said solemnly, as he pulled up a chair at the table and began helping himself to breakfast cereal.

'I'm moving into my new place as soon as I finish work today.'

'I see' I said. 'I hope you'll be comfortable there, Peter.'

'So do I' he said. 'I'll phone you in a few days.'

'Good' I said. 'Will you be leaving a contact number with us?'

'No' he said firmly. 'I've just told you I'll phone you in a few days.'

I'd got it wrong again. I poured myself another cup of tea and began looking at the morning paper. It was best to ignore him.

He made himself toast and poured himself a cup of tea. I could feel his eyes on me but continued to ignore him.

He finished his breakfast. 'You and Dad can have your lives back now that I'm going.'

'Yes, we can Peter' I said. 'We've all had a hard few months, but it is getting better.'

'Do you think so?' he said.

I detected a hint of sincere questioning in his voice, as though he needed some additional reassurance before he left to face his new challenge.

'Yes, Peter' I said. 'I really do.'

He smiled. 'Good' he said getting up. 'I'm off then.'

'OK Peter' I said, hesitating briefly before getting up too and following him out of the house to his car.

'Bye then' he said. He got into his car and slammed the door. He switched on the engine and drove away. His parting was as simple and unemotional as that. Not a peck on the cheek or a hug. Just 'Bye then.'

I walked back into the house, went straight to his room and sat on his bed. I felt neither joy nor sorrow as I looked around me. I just felt nothing. I had wondered over the months that Peter was with us, that if ever he was well enough to leave, I would feel a wonderful sense of freedom and relief because John and I would have our lives back to call our own. Do as we pleased. But I felt nothing. Nothing at all. I was completely wrung out.

Inevitably, there would be more to face in time. Since Peter's diagnosis I had been well aware of that. But the intensity of emotion I had experienced and come through had been such that I knew as I sat on the bed that from then on, whatever happened, I would somehow be equipped to cope.

I was still lost in thought when the phone rang and jolted me back to reality. It was John.

'Hello love' he said. 'Has Peter gone?'

'Yes. He went ages ago. I haven't done a thing since he left except sit on his bed. I haven't even cleared the breakfast. I've no idea what time it is.'

He chuckled, 'I'm not surprised. It's all a bit of an anti-climax really.'

'I know. What time will you be home?'

'Late afternoon; and we are going out for a meal tonight, to celebrate. I think we deserve it. I'll book a table. Bye for now.'

I put the phone down and went back to Peter's room. I stripped his bed, took down the curtains and turned the mattress.

The following day, I replaced all the original bed covers and curtains and the room was just as it had been in the October of the previous year.

And so our longed-for normality began, although we both knew that we would feel much more comfortable once Peter had been in touch.

It was almost a week after he had moved out before Peter phoned and invited us to see where he was living. I had jumped every time the phone had rung, anxious to hear that all was well, even though I knew that he was much better.

John and I drove over to Skipton that weekend and were pleasantly surprised to see that he had found himself some very comfortable accommodation.

He had rented a bed-sitting room on the ground floor of a large Victorian house, and shared the kitchen and bathroom with the other residents, a policeman and a young woman who worked as a secretary. Peter told us that they were very friendly and that he was coping well. He appeared to be very pleased with himself and surprised us by insisting he made us a cup of tea. As he handed it to us, he chuckled and said,

'I bet you're glad I've moved out.'

John and I just smiled and nodded.

The house was ten minutes walking distance from Jonathan's shop and Peter was appreciating not having to drive half an hour to work each day.

Coming to Terms

He was still seeing the specialist once a month at that time.

CHAPTER 20

July 1996 – December 1998

Over the following months, it was very noticeable that Peter's new circumstances and routine were doing wonders for his confidence. Every few days he would invite us over to see him although when we did so, we kept our visits short. He was more relaxed in himself, and it was as though he just wanted to reassure us that all was well. His manner had become polite rather than hostile, although he still lacked the warmth that had always been part of his nature. He spent as much time as he could with Jane and was pleased when a close friend of hers rented the house next door to her, for he was far from happy that Jane was living alone.

We phoned Jane every few days and I would regularly drive over to see her.

Just as Dr Patra had predicted, she was mentally stable – enjoying her pregnancy and counting the weeks and days to the birth of the baby.

Another turning point came when she was admitted to hospital with chest pains early in November, just eight weeks before the baby was due. She had developed blood clots in her lungs. She was treated successfully and Peter had by then been concerned, attentive and responsible for three months and so she suggested that he move in with her when she was discharged from hospital.

Peter was absolutely delighted. He moved in with his belongings and very happily drove her home from hospital a week later.

Jane gave birth to a little girl on New Years Eve. They named her Kayleigh Jane.

Coming to Terms

As soon as we heard the news, John and I drove over to see her and the proud new parents. They were absolutely ecstatic over their little girl, and seeing them both so very happy was wonderful, after all that we had seen them suffer.

In a very short space of time they settled into a domestic routine, as caring for their little girl who had given them the focus they had so badly needed consumed their lives. When we visited, Peter was still quiet with us, but he proved to be a wonderful father, and seeing him at last so contented with his new life more than compensated. Jane went out of her way to make us feel welcome, encouraged our visits, and motherhood suited her.

In contrast to the pressures and stresses of the previous three years, the freedom John and I felt at that time was wonderful and we took full advantage of it as we caught up with so much that had hitherto been on hold. A long overdue visit to Cornwall to see Mike, Zoe and Jacob was first on our agenda, followed by a week in Madeira, and Paris. We enjoyed other short weekend breaks, and appreciated and enjoyed rebuilding the social life we had missed. We also began involving ourselves once more in the numerous village activities.

Over the months that followed, Peter was so contented that gradually his attitude towards John and I began to change. We began to feel more and more comfortable in each other's company and he began to phone us occasionally to tell us of Kayleigh's development; he was so very proud of her. He was better, but not surprisingly he was no longer the Peter we remembered. However, it had to be good enough. He had found that life was, after all, worth living.

In May, Peter, Jane and Kayleigh, then just five months old, and Mike and Zoe with Jacob who was then just two, joined us for a holiday in Scotland and we all had a wonderful time. Jane and I had become very close by then and still talked regularly on the telephone. But a call from her late that summer with the kind of news that was to bring about another testing time for them, served as a reminder of how changeable life could suddenly be.

'We've had a terrible shock, Arlene.' Then she said 'Jonathan has made Peter redundant.'

I collapsed into the hall chair, heart thumping fast again.

'But he can't have, Jane. He was doing so well.'

'Yes, I know. We're baffled. Jonathan won't tell Peter why. He just says it's financial.'

'But Peter has worked so hard for Jonathan.'

'I know, but Peter went into work this morning and his desk had been cleared and that was it.'

'How has Peter taken it?'

'Amazingly well really. I thought he'd be in a terrible state but he doesn't seem to be over-bothered. I can't understand it really. He's been so happy over the last few months. Jonathan just keeps saying it's financial and that's the only reason he's giving.'

We were completely bewildered and still are to this day as to why Peter was given his notice. John went so far as to phone Jonathan and learned nothing more than Peter had already been told. We have pondered over it many times since and the only conclusion we have reached is that Peter was so happy and confident at that time that possibly he was on a 'high' and perhaps might have been careless at times and flippant with customers. Jonathan, not wanting to cause any upset in the family, had perhaps felt that he had taken the diplomatic route.

Coming to Terms

Whether we were right or not we will never know.

But I believe that everything in life happens for a reason and this was no exception, for within a couple of weeks, Peter had managed to find a job in administration in a large printing works in Halifax. It proved to be a good move, for again Peter was working in an environment in which he had had experience, and also he was working closer to home and there was much less travelling each day.

Over the following first few months of that year, life couldn't have been happier for Peter and Jane and indeed the whole family. We spent many happy times with them and they would frequently call over to see us. We doted on our little granddaughter, as we did Jacob, although distance prevented us seeing and enjoying him as much as we would have liked.

But nothing lasts forever. It had been a long time since Peter and Jane had given us cause for concern, so it came as a shock to notice when we were with them signs that they were no longer happy and relaxed with one another. There were atmospheres when we visited them and a sadness had begun to envelop them both.

Coincidentally, the printing firm that Peter was working for began falling apart, and Peter was made redundant yet again. As if that were not enough, we were to learn that Jane was expecting another baby at the end of the year. Once again we had to pretend we were happy for them.

I observed them carefully when we were with them and I felt that neither of them was depressed in the sense that they were both bipolar sufferers. Even if my assumption was wrong, at least it was comforting to know that Jane's pregnancy would carry her through whatever was at the root of these unhappy circumstances. If Peter was down he would be no use to her at all. But I was not convinced that he was clinically depressed.

John and I tried to pretend all this was not happening and lived in hope that Kayleigh and the expected baby would be a bond that would keep Peter and Jane together. All we could do was wait and see.

Peter, against all odds, managed to find another job, this time with a telephone sales company. The pay was poor and the work a far cry from anything he had done before. They were struggling to make ends meet and Jane began working a few hours a week as a receptionist for a friend who had a hairdressing business. Sue, the friend who lived next door, looked after Kayleigh for a few hours each week and, desperate to help, I too would drive over once a week, pick her up and bring her home to us for an overnight stay.

They were grim days and although Peter and Jane were making the best of things in the practical sense, it was clear that they were growing apart.

As Jane spent more and more time with Sue, Peter became jealous. Feeling isolated and seeking company, he began drinking at every opportunity with money they could ill afford.

CHAPTER 21

January 1999

Jane gave birth to another little girl on January 4th. They named her Sinead. This time there was no real joy. Just a relief that Jane's pregnancy was over.

A short time later the situation was made worse. When the baby was just six weeks old, Peter, unable to cope with the pressure of telephone selling and fearing that the stress would trigger a more serious bipolar depression, handed in his notice.

They then began living on unemployment benefit. He had also begun drinking again.

My heart bled for them both. We pitied Jane who was reaching the point of desperation. Coping with the baby and the additional worry of Peter's irresponsible and irrational behaviour was taking its toll on her.

Angry though we were with him for drinking, we realised he was again beyond reasoning and lived in terrible fear of the consequences.

The situation continued to worsen, and the more Jane relied on Sue for comfort and support, the more Peter leaned on alcohol. He did try to get work and went for interviews but always failed them, miserably.

John and I never gave up hope that the children would finally bind Peter and Jane together.

But our hopes were dashed one Monday morning at the end of March, just a few days before my Mother's eightieth birthday.

John and I were due to travel down to Norwich to stay with her for the weekend. I had had a cake made and iced and together with my brothers and their wives, we were taking mother out for a celebration lunch. She was looking forward to it greatly. Naturally, my mother knew about Peter and would frequently ask after him, especially during the time he had been with us and so ill. I would tell her only as much as she needed to know to keep her from worrying and had become adept at telling her white lies, although I didn't doubt for a minute that she could sense I was doing so. Never was my deception to be so thoroughly tested than after the news I was to learn from Jane when I picked up the phone that morning.

'Hello Arlene. It's Jane.' She said it in such a businesslike voice, I knew in an instant that something was seriously wrong.

'Hello Jane. What is it? What's the matter?'

'I'm ringing to tell you that Peter and I are separating.'

I was stunned into silence as I struggled to take in her words.

'Are you still there, Arlene?' Jane asked.

'Yes, I am Jane. And I'm so, so sorry. It's such a shock. Are you both absolutely sure about this?'

My words must have sounded mournful, I was so shaken, yet I knew that whatever I said would make no difference.

'Oh yes. I'm sorry too Arlene, but I just can't cope any more living like this. I'm going over to my mother with the girls to give Peter time to sort himself out and find somewhere to live. I'll be back at the weekend.'

I was tempted to ask whether this was to be a trial

separation, then thought better of it, for I knew deep down that this was it. Our little family was to be no more.

'Is there anything at all that we can do, Jane'? I said hopefully.

'Not really. But I know I can call on you.'

'Where is Peter now, Jane?'

'He's gone for a walk. I expect he'll be talking to you later. Bye for now, Arlene' and she put down the phone.

Jane had never spoken to me in that tone before and it hurt. We all knew her well enough to know that blocking out emotion was her way of coping. Not totally surprised and unable to move, I sat for what seemed an eternity, staring out of the window at that grey morning. This was going to be another crossroads in their lives, as if they hadn't already been through enough. This time there were children involved, the challenge ahead of them far greater than either of them had had to face before. As I sat there, I remembered the anguish Peter had suffered over losing Sarah and the times without number that he said that he had nothing to live for. This time he was losing not only Jane who had been his saviour, but he would never, from then on, share a home with his little girls.

As I thought of all that they had had and all that might have been and of those poor children, and of the gravity of this new and terrible situation, tears began to stream down my face, and I howled out loud.

CHAPTER 22

April 1999

Before John and I left for Norwich, we tried several times to contact Peter and left messages on the phone, but he never replied. We concluded that he didn't want to trouble us and hoped that he was just busy trying to find somewhere to live. Although remembering how he had been when he and Sarah had separated, it was hard not to think the worst as we journeyed down that Friday afternoon.

Against all odds, John and I both managed to put up a cheery facade for my mother, who enjoyed her weekend celebration greatly. She had been widowed very young, had had a hard life and so well deserved her treat, and the many presents, flowers and gifts she received from friends as well as family, so we were all very happy for her. Perhaps relaxing with easy company was just what we needed before facing up to more stress once we were home again. But Peter was never far from our minds.

Late afternoon on the day of our return, I was unpacking when I heard John answer the phone but forced myself to continue what I was doing, fearful of what I would be about to hear. I knew he was talking to Jane and the tone of his voice was such that it was clear that all was not well. The call over, John came into the bedroom and sat down on the bed. He patted the bed beside where he was sitting, indicating that I should sit with him. I did so, then I took a deep breath and clenching my fists and closing my eyes, braced myself for what I was to hear.

This new situation was so awful that I knew that whatever was happening, Peter would be in a terrible state and he still hadn't been in touch with us.

Coming to Terms

'Jane says that when she got back from her mother's, Peter took the car and he drove to their local. He's drunk and asleep in the car in the car park.'

'And what about Jane and the children?'

'She says she's as right as she can be. Her mother has been helping and so has Sue. She says she has other friends she can call on. We're not to worry about her, but she thought she ought to let us know about Peter because there's no way he can go back there.'

We sat there side by side for some time digesting what we had just heard.

'We'll have to go over there, John. He'll end up in the gutter.'

'I know. But I'm going on my own. I don't want you to come and see him like this. I'll go over and sober him up and see what I can do. You've been upset enough. Prepare yourself though in case I bring him back with me. I'll go straight away.'

I finished unpacking and made up a bed for Peter, not doubting for a moment that John would bring him home. I was angry with Peter for being so irresponsible, and trying to imagine him living a life without Jane and his little girls was incomprehensible.

John arrived back late that night alone. He had found Peter in a pitiful state, slumped in the car, unshaven, dirty, carelessly dressed and reeking of alcohol. He had taken him to a cafe where, after a couple of black coffees, he had begun to talk coherently.

Peter told him that he had spent the previous few days walking the streets of Halifax trying to find somewhere to live but had not managed to do so. In desperation, he had been to the Samaritans who had recommended an address but there were no vacancies. He had been to Social Services and also registered at the Job Centre but they had nothing to offer him. He had tried everything and got nowhere. Completely defeated, he had used up the remains of his money to drink and shut out his misery.

He was adamant that he didn't want to come home to us but he had agreed to come back with John to Harrogate. In the back of the car was a large bag in which Peter said was a change of clothing and his toiletries.

John had then phoned Jane to let her know. Saddened but relieved, she told John that she had spare keys to the car and that she would arrange to have it picked up. Reassuring her that we would be in touch, John then drove back to Harrogate where he booked Peter into bed and breakfast accommodation for the following week and left him with enough money to get through and collect his thoughts. There he hoped Peter would have time, in comfortable circumstances at least, to think about all he had to face.

In the meantime, Peter had agreed to register at the Job Centre in Harrogate, and although John had grave doubts as to whether he was in a fit state to start work, he felt that he should be given another opportunity to try.

Black days were with us again. We heard nothing from Peter over the following days. I feared for him and his mental state. Clearly he was ill and down again and I desperately wanted him home, where I could keep a careful eye on him as I had done years before. My sleepless nights were back as I would lie awake thinking of him, his plight, and of Jane and the children.

The weather through those early days in April was wet, miserable and very cold. So anxious did I become, that when shopping in town one day I walked and walked through a snow blizzard, visualising Peter trailing round the town wet and miserable, hoping against hope that by chance I would meet up with him and persuade him to come home with me. I just knew that he needed serious help and that he would not succeed on his own. Also, I knew that my instinct had never let me down.

I was to see proof of it five days after John had left Peter in Harrogate.

It was another wet evening. I was preparing our meal when to my astonishment Peter walked through the kitchen door.

He was soaked and looked absolutely frozen. I stood transfixed. I had never ever seen him looking so wretched. Without a word he dropped his holdall onto the floor, pulled out a chair, undid his jacket zip then slowly and wearily sat down and put his head in his hands. He tried to speak but his words wouldn't come. He looked up at me and a vision flashed through my mind of the little boy in my dream. I walked over and cradled his head in my arms as he let go and cried and cried.

'I'm sorry, Mum.'

'It's all right Peter. I'm glad you've come home.'

'I've tried so hard. I was determined not to bother you and Dad again. I ran out of money so I slept in a hostel with down and outs last night.'

I turned my face away so that he couldn't see my look of horror.

'I couldn't sleep and kept thinking about my little girls. I feel I don't want to go on any more, Mum. But I've got to for them.'

Almost overcome with emotion and again not wanting

Peter to see, I turned to the sink and began scraping peelings into the bin. I took a deep breath.

'You must be hungry.'

I helped him off with his coat.

He nodded. 'I haven't eaten since last night.'

'Why don't you have a soak in the bath whilst I get on with dinner? Your Dad will be home soon. I think he'll be glad to see you too. We've been so worried about you.'

'OK. Thanks Mum.'

He slowly dragged himself back onto his feet and walked through into the hall and up to the bathroom. I picked up his sodden jacket and hung it in the utility room and put his shoes on the floor near the boiler as I heard him running the bath.

As I did all this, I thought of the time he had come to us after his first breakdown, and wondered just how much more misery would envelop him before he came through, and how on earth he would cope with this new and seemingly insurmountable challenge.

CHAPTER 23

May 1999

It was patently clear that Peter needed more help and support than we could give him. We made an appointment for him to see Dr Patra, who decided not to admit him but arranged for Peter to have a month's course of treatment and counselling, commencing the next day.

Peter was to attend the clinic each day from 9am to 5pm for the first two weeks and then for three days a week for the remainder of the month.

I arranged with Jane that I would pick up the children and bring them over every few days so that Peter could continue to see them. She assured us that she was managing and chose not to call upon us for help. She told us that for the time being she would prefer to be independent. Our relationship with her became very strained and, having been close to her, I missed her dreadfully.

Peter soon settled into a routine and although he was quiet, we had no problem with having him stay with us.

After his first week at the clinic he began to look better. He would go off for walks but I no longer worried that he might not come back. He lived for his days with the children in whose company he became transformed.

Peter missed Jane but rarely mentioned her name or talked to us about her in the way that he had over Sarah. This time he was suffering far more deeply.

He began telling us about his days at the clinic, praising the staff, and of friends he was making with some of the other patients on the course. Learning of their sad circumstances and histories seemed to give Peter the comparison and motivation he needed and had been lacking.

Towards the end of his time at the clinic Peter began to look for accommodation in Harrogate and rented an attic room in a shared house just on the outskirts of town. All he had was a double bed, a wardrobe, a chest of drawers and a chair. But he was pleased with himself and saw this as the beginning of a new life.

His course at the clinic completed, Peter's confidence grew as did his determination. He would speak to Jane to make arrangements regarding the children, and thankfully there was no animosity. They were just pleasantly polite with one another. We helped him with the children and would frequently have them stay overnight. After a month, Peter felt that he could manage them himself. He slept head-to-toe in the double bed with Kayleigh who thought it a great treat; whilst Sinead slept happily in her carry-cot at the foot of the bed. How he managed the bottle feeds and nappies with the kitchen and bathroom two floors down, amazed us.

As Peter continued to improve, he called daily at the Job Centre and as no suitable work was available at that time, on the recommendation of the Citizens Advice Bureau he began calling daily at The Harrogate East Parade Project which is a drop-in and social centre for the young and unemployed. There, within days, he began helping the office staff produce the monthly magazine, also writing and contributing an article himself.

Praised and encouraged by the staff at the East Parade Project after all he had achieved, he began again applying for various jobs, but his experience of the previous years impacted upon his ability to project himself and his capabilities at interview. But he never, ever gave up. His determination never faltered.

Finally, his perseverance was rewarded. At the end of July he was offered a job as a trainee chef in the kitchen of a large hotel in Harrogate.

He was delighted and enthusiastic. He had always liked cooking, and although he had never considered working professionally in kitchens, thought that this might well be his future path. John and I encouraged him, although we had misgivings as to whether the inevitable stress of working in what would be bound to be a hectically busy environment would be right for him.

Within the first couple of weeks the strain was beginning to show and Peter admitted to having had his first binge in months. Angry with himself, he was determined to continue trying to deal with the pressure of the daily unrelenting routine, although the harder he tried, the more stressed he became.

John and I watched Peter very carefully and wouldn't have been in the least surprised if he had handed in his notice, in fact we hoped that he would do so. But as if he hadn't already been through enough, he had yet another set back.

CHAPTER 24

June 1999

One morning when Peter had been working in the kitchen for just three weeks, I had a phone call.

'Is that Mrs. Hindle?'

'Yes it is.'

'I'm a male staff-nurse at the district hospital. I'm sorry to have to tell you that your son, Peter, has had a nasty scalding accident and is here in casualty. He's asked me to let you know.'

I closed my eyes, took a deep breath, in readiness for more.

'How? When? How badly is he scalded?'

'It happened in the kitchen at the hotel this morning. He was brought in by ambulance.'

A vision crossed my mind of the horrendous sights I had seen as a student nurse, in a burns unit I had worked in through my hospital training.

'Thank you for letting me know.' I said 'Tell Peter I will come straight there.'

I decided not to phone John until I knew more and had been to the hospital. I worked yet again at concentrating on staying calm as I drove there, and it crossed my mind what a typical manic depressive Peter seemed to be. I had read that for some strange unexplained reason they could be accident prone. At the same time I recalled his attitude towards me at the time of his head injury. I wondered how he would be this time.

Peter appeared to be relieved to see me as I was led into his cubicle in casualty; he even managed a smile as I approached him. The nurse said that someone would be along to see me very soon.

The first thing I noticed was the raw, red scald over his eye.

'Hello Mum' he said. 'Thank you for coming. I knew you would. Don't look so worried. I'll be all right.'

His speech was slurred with the effects of the pain killers.

I composed myself as I adjusted to these new and alarming circumstances. Every few seconds or so, Peter would close his eyes and frown as he inhaled from the gas and air mask he had also been given to relieve his pain. He had an intravenous drip in his arm.

'What on earth happened, Peter?'

I was anxious to see the extent of his injuries and gently lifted the sheet that was draped over a long cage, placed over the length of his body and as I looked and listened I could feel his eyes on me.

'I slipped and fell in the kitchen at work and knocked over a big pan of boiling water. I landed flat on my back and it poured all over me.'

I momentarily closed my eyes and tried to imagine the pain. Practically the whole of the front of his body was covered in dressings, also both his thighs and his right arm.

'Don't worry, Mum. They've been really kind to me here. I'll be all right.' He closed his eyes and inhaled more gas and air.

'It's madness in that kitchen. Everybody dashing about. Especially in the mornings. The floor was wet as well.'

'Don't talk any more, Peter.' I said. 'Just close your eyes for a while.'

I pulled up a chair, and sat down beside him, again wondering how much more he would have to suffer, before he would begin to get some kind of life together. Also I thought about our misgivings about the work in the kitchen.

Peter eventually dozed off. I sat watching him, listening to the noises in the background. Casualty was busy.

Eventually, a male staff nurse appeared and introduced himself as the one who had phoned me. He said that they were waiting for an ambulance to take Peter to the burns unit at Pinderfields Hospital in Wakefield. The casualty doctor felt that the extent of Peter's skin damage needed to be assessed as he might need skin grafts. We wouldn't have much longer to wait as Peter was an urgent case.

Peter opened his eyes and took all this in. The analgesics were taking effect and he looked more relaxed. But I then had some clear thinking to do. I was worried that if I went with Peter in the ambulance, in all probability I would have to make my own way home. I had no idea of the location of Pinderfields and was wondering how I would get back and what to do, when Peter said,

'Don't worry, Mum. You needn't come with me. If I have to stay there you can come down with Dad tomorrow.'

Incredibly, despite all he was going through, Peter had read my thoughts and was again reassuring me.

Coming to Terms

Please, Mum. I'm going to need your help when I get back. You know that.'

He dozed off again and I stayed with him until the ambulance arrived. The crew were careful and kind as they transferred Peter into the ambulance. He managed another smile as I wished him luck and waved him off.

I drove home upset and worried, but thinking how much Peter's attitude towards me had changed since his head injury accident just two years previously. No matter what the outcome of his accident, this time caring for him would be infinitely more tolerable.

The news was good when I phoned Pinderfields Hospital later that day. The skin specialist had concluded that Peter would not need any skin grafting. He had been started on a course of antibiotics and he was to have his scalds dressed daily for the next two weeks, after which he wanted to see Peter again. The scarring, in time, would be negligible.

After an overnight stay at Pinderfields where he was kept under observation for shock, Peter was transferred back to Harrogate for a further two days and then discharged home. John and I suggested he might like to come and stay with us again but he thanked us and refused. He was adamant that he wanted to try and continue to manage on his own, although he had been told that it would be a month at least before he could consider going back to work.

I was in for a big surprise when I asked him about the arrangements for his daily dressings.

'They were going to send a district nurse, Mum. But I told them not to worry, that you used to be a nurse and that I would rather you did them for me.'

'Really?' I said. I can remember laughing.

'What did they say? Didn't they mind?'

'Not in the least. In fact, the doctor was quite pleased. He said the district nurses would be as well.'

I confess I was pleased too, not only because I was keen to help Peter in some way but also because this was a most wonderful indication that he had such faith in me.

And so it was that each day for the next two weeks I dressed Peter's scalds. He had been discharged with a huge bag of dressings. There was specially impregnated gauze, mountains of plain white hospital gauze, cotton wool, a huge pile of assorted bandages, saline packs, scissors and disposable forceps, together with strong pain killers. But challenging though it was for both of us, the bond that developed between Peter and I over that time was something I have never, ever forgotten.

I had to brace myself for what I was to see, as I set about peeling off the gauze for the very first time. I had dressed many wounds over my nursing years and liked to think that I had coped efficiently and kindly. This time I had to consider, control and hide my emotion too, as Peter, despite having taken his pain-killers in good time before I began, would still suffer unavoidable pain, as I did all that there was to do.

It took well over an hour to dress his wounds each day. But as the wounds began to heal, Peter's pain began to ease, and we developed a manageable routine that became a therapy for us both, Peter talking and telling me his worries and heartaches as I worked.

The specialist was pleased with Peter's progress and as the wounds continued to heal, the dressings were reduced until they became negligible. There were nevertheless several huge scars, though in time, as the specialist had predicted, they began to fade.

By the time Peter had recovered sufficiently to start work again he was seriously worried, and fearful of going back to work in the kitchen.

He gave it a try but was so nervous that he found it quite impossible to work there and after just three days, handed in his notice.

CHAPTER 25

July to November 1999

Peter's attic life continued as before. A daily visit to the Job Centre and the East Parade where project staff were always glad of his help. As always, time with his girls was his most precious commodity. He hated being on unemployment benefit but was never too proud to try anything to earn money. For a few weeks he walked miles and miles posting leaflets through doors for an estate agent and joked that he knew every street and road in Harrogate. So keen was he to begin work that he thought nothing of asking to see company managers face to face, asking if they had anything at all to offer. He never became despondent or gave up trying, until finally he successfully applied for an office job with a small printing company, the only drawback being that the office was some twenty miles out of town.

The job involved working in an office with an elderly female employee who had been with the company for many years and was very reserved. Peter found her difficult company as she barely spoke and because of this he felt that she was making no effort to help him settle into the work and routine, which was hard for him, as he was feeling particularly sensitive at that time and had little confidence. The job description had also been misleading, for although Peter had been told that there would be some driving involved, there was much more than he had been led to believe. At first, he enjoyed being away from the office and delivering orders in the many beautiful areas on the North Yorkshire moors in fine weather, but as winter began to set in with its dark days, the driving became a nightmare and he began once more to feel lonely and isolated. The crunch finally came, when late one afternoon, he got hopelessly lost in thick fog for hours, miles from anywhere. He very wisely handed in his notice the following day.

Coming to Terms

Still undeterred, Peter continued seeking work and looked upon the search as a job in itself.

His patience was finally rewarded at the beginning of November, seven months after his separation from Jane.

He had seen an advert for a path. lab. assistant at the Harrogate District Hospital and applied.

For the first time in months, his hopes were raised as he went along for an interview. Considering his complaint, his long and complicated employment history, and also the competition there would be, John and I felt that the likelihood of Peter being offered the job was remote but we admired his optimism and wished him luck. After all his stoical efforts over many months he, more than most, deserved to be rewarded.

Peter wasn't offered the job, was disappointed and admitted to us later that he hadn't been totally surprised but had felt that the experience of the interview had been good for him. But that day Peter did indeed get his reward.

Whilst he was there at the hospital, he learned that there was a vacancy for a hospital porter. He made further enquiries, and was given an application form. An interview two days later sealed his fate. Providing he passed a thorough medical examination, he had a job.

It was as though this was all too good to be true for Peter. After all his bad luck, he worried about whether the fact that he was a manic depressive would stand in his way. He passed his physical and on the medical examiners recommendation was to have a three month trial, and then a re-assessment.

In due course he passed this too and has been working at the hospital ever since.

Peter started work at the hospital in November 1999, almost seven years to the day since he had come home to us after his first breakdown.

Seven years during which he had lived through a lifetime.

He was nervous at first, wondering how he would cope with working with the general public again.

After the first week he was phoning us, enthusing about the job and all that it entailed. Within a month he was happily settled into the routine and had no problem at all deciding to rent a small but adequate ground floor flat just ten minutes walk from the hospital.

Peter has never considered going back into the printing industry, mainly we believe, because it has so many unhappy memories for him.

He has been working at the hospital for almost eight years now. There have been times when he has felt that the work wasn't giving him the mental stimulus he needed. Recognising this, he applied himself to a number of courses, gaining the European Computer Driving Licence, a Public Health and Hygiene Certificate and also has a qualification in sign language. He works hard and is popular, having regained his confidence and his sense of humour.

He has also recognised that in order to remain stable and manage his complaint, work must be, in the main, stress free, and in a varied working environment.

He still sees his girls on alternate weekends and during school holidays and lives for them. Each summer he takes them down to Cornwall for a week's holiday with Mike and his family.

Peter has a very amicable relationship with Jane. She has

had two bouts of depression since she and Peter parted and was readmitted to the clinic on both occasions. Despite their separation they both consider their time together, particularly in the early days after their diagnosis, to have been invaluable and a huge learning curve for them both. They have never forgotten the months they travelled the long and wearisome road together as they worked their way through accepting their diagnosis and fighting off their demons.

Jane will always be special to John and I, and not only because she is the mother of our granddaughters, for, without her, we doubt very much whether Peter would have come through. On reflection, we perhaps leaned on her too heavily, realising how valuable she had become to us all. She gave Peter a focus when he had thought for so long that life was not worth living. Suffering her own severe depression, she selflessly concentrated on helping Peter and she became an indispensable part of his life.

Peter, John and I love her dearly and will be endlessly grateful to her.

Peter is stable on Lithium, and has taken it conscientiously ever since his diagnosis. He has a blood test every six months to check his Lithium levels and also sees Dr Patra every three months. He rarely touches alcohol, and gets furious when he notices people at social occasions who are 'worse for wear'. He says it is because seeing them reminds him of the way he used to be. He also knows that alcohol will cancel out his Lithium.

Peter, at long last, appears to be very contented with his life. He is always most considerate of John and I, and once again we all enjoy each others' company greatly.

But Peter's story doesn't quite end there. For as though it were necessary for us to be always aware that the complaint would never quite go away, Peter went 'down' again four years after he started work at the hospital.

He phoned us one evening early in January, to tell us that he didn't feel right.

'I don't want to get up in the mornings and my appetite has gone. I'm managing to work but I'm feeling anxious all the time and I'm short tempered.'

I asked him how long he had felt like that.

'Nearly a week. But I've been thinking about it and I've felt ever so happy and optimistic about everything on and off for the last month so I think I must have been high. It's frightened me really. So I've made an appointment to see Dr Patra tomorrow.'

Peter had been very wise and he had also been right.

He was down again.

Dr Patra recommended that Peter should come home to us and stay until the depression had passed. He had no doubt in his mind that it would.

Peter came back and stayed with us for two months. But how very different it was having him live with us that time. The signs and symptoms of depression were all there again but this time he was overwhelmingly appreciative of all that we did for him as he worked his way through his depression. Never, for a moment, was he unpleasant to us and between us we managed to cope, although as before, it was hard seeing him suffer. Not once did he say that he had nothing to live for. For this time he had his girls, who we made sure he saw just for a couple of hours each week.

Seven weeks after he had been with us, Peter said one morning, 'I'm going back to work.'

He still looked ill and we had seen few real signs that he was getting better, although we knew it would be futile to discourage him.

'Please don't worry about me' he said. 'I've got to try. I'll get through. I have to.'

A week later he moved out and back to his flat, promising that he would phone us every day; and so he did.

Peter managed to work through his depression although it was a hard, uphill climb for him and almost six months until he was well again. He would work himself to exhaustion, then spend the whole of his free time curled up in bed, shutting out the world. The staff at the hospital were very understanding and kind, recognising his need to persevere.

His girls gave him the motivation he needed. In their blind innocence, they got him through.

He has been fine ever since.

I have written this story with Peter's blessing.

Postscript August 2008

Three years after Jane and Peter separated, Jane married Neil, a friend of long-standing, and there are two little boys by that marriage.

Neil has proved to be a wonderful stepfather to Kayleigh and Sinead.

Tragically, Jane was diagnosed as having bone cancer in the Spring of 2007. Having suffered cruelly, and losing her battle to survive for her children, she died a year later.

Our heartache has been huge.

After Jane's death, it was jointly decided to keep the four children together with Neil. He has a great deal of support, practically and financially, and copes extremely well.

Peter and Neil signed a legal joint guardianship agreement.

Peter continues to have his girls stay on a regular basis and remains stable.

Jane is very much missed. As John once said, 'She came into our lives like an angel'.

Bipolar Disorder

Bipolar Disorder or Manic Depression as it was once mainly called is about mood swings caused by an imbalance in the brain chemistry that can lead to states of great euphoria, manic acts, or severe depression.

Without doubt, it is a most frightening complaint for those severely affected.

Some sufferers can incur literally thousands of pounds of debt on wild and irresponsible spending sprees. Or they indulge in totally outrageous uncontrollable acts, the aftermath of which can also be devastating. In contrast, there can be utter desolation and complete lack of a will to live. 5% of people diagnosed with Bipolar Disorder take their own lives.

For those less severely affected, an occasional bout of depression, lasting just a few days or weeks, may be the pattern, or there may be just short periods of dramatic, irrational behaviour, nonetheless upsetting in its aftermath.

Over several years now, a great deal of research has revealed that if diagnosed correctly, the complaint can be treated, and in a great number of cases very successfully, with Lithium, a chemical that was discovered in 1949 by John Cade, an Australian psychiatrist. He proved that it calmed manic patients.
Lithium is a natural element rather like sodium in table salt and is found in certain rocks, mineral waters and plants, and is also present in the human body in minute amounts although it has no known function and is not considered to be essential for normal health.

At first, results and conclusions were treated with scepticism. However, further research over the years proved that measured doses of Lithium can indeed be invaluable in maintaining a chemical balance in the brain, essential in preventing severe mood swings. Now it is used universally in the treatment of manic depression.

Those fortunate enough to respond well to the treatment enjoy a good quality of life, providing that they take the medication conscientiously, and have regular blood tests to ensure that the Lithium balance is maintained at a satisfactory therapeutic level.

Bipolar Disorder is mainly genetic and results have shown that where there appears to be a tendency to the complaint within a family, the response to Lithium is much better.

Nowadays, there are available other medications that are used successfully in treating Bipolar Disorder as research in medicine and mental illness continues.

For those unfortunates who do not respond so well to medication, life is a long tortuous path dogged time and time again by the cruel effects of the ever-changing mood swings and sudden, uncontrollable behaviour. So wearisome, that for the next of kin watching by helplessly, the complaint at times must almost seem to be contagious.

As his story has revealed, Peter is a true 'text book' manic depressive.

This is evidenced if we reflect back on Peter's highs when he met Sarah, his irresponsible spending and irrational behaviour, which lead to those unpaid bills, and then his plunge into serious depression.

Also I referred early in the story to the fact that John's brother took his life, and that the family has never known why. He was apparently prone to moods, but he never sought help. I have always believed since Peter's diagnosis, and the fact that the complaint is genetic, that it is highly probable that John's brother might possibly have had Bipolar Disorder too.

www.ingramcontent.com/pod-product-compliance
Lightning Source LLC
Chambersburg PA
CBHW021157010426
R18062100001B/R180621PG41931CBX00005B/7

* 9 7 8 1 8 4 9 9 1 4 9 3 2 *